Theology and the Body

edited by

Stephen Garner

Theology and the Body

Reflections on Being Flesh and Blood

edited by

Stephen Garner

2011

Interface: A Forum for Theology in the World

Volume 14, Number 2 2011

Interface is an ecumenical and interdisciplinary theological journal dealing with issues of a social and cultural nature.
Interface is an independently refereed journal.

Editor in Chief: Revd Dr Paul Babie, Adelaide University, Adelaide
Revd Dr John Capper, Tabor College, Melbourne
Revd Malcolm Coombes, Trinity Theological College, Brisbane
Dr Anne Hunt, Australian Catholic University, Melbourne
Dr Philip Kariatlis, St Andrew's Greek Orthodox College, Sydney
Dr Jo Laffin, Catholic Theological College, Flinders University/Adelaide College of Divinity, Adelaide
Revd Dr Tim Meadowcroft, Laidlaw College, Auckland, New Zealand
Revd Dr Denis Minns OP, Catholic Institute of Sydney, Sydney
Revd Dr Jeff Silcock, Australian Lutheran College, Adelaide

Mailing address:
Interface, PO Box 504, Hindmarsh, SA 5007
email: hdregan@atf.org.au
ATF Home Page: www.atf.org.au

Subscription Rates (2010)
Australia: Individual Aus $55 p/a (includes GST)
           Institutional Aus $85 p/a (includes GST)
Overseas: Individual and institutions Aus $95 p/a

Electronic subscriptions available.

Send all subscriptions to:
Interface
PO Box 504
Hindmarsh SA 5007

Interface is published by the ATF Theology an imprint of ATF (Australia)Ltd (ABN 90 116 359 963) and is published in May and October of each year.
Interface is indexed in the *Australasian Religion Index*
ISSN 1329-6264

© Copyright
This publication is copyright. Apart from any fair dealing for the purposes of private study, research, criticism or review, as permitted under the Copyright Act, no part may be reproduced by any process without written permission.

Table of Contents

Editorial	vii
A Theology of the Body: Pope John Paul II's Catechetical Lectures *Adam G Cooper*	1
Blood, Tears and Race: Moravian Missionaries and Indigenous Bodies in Colonial Australia *Joanna Cruickshank*	15
Image-bearing cyborgs? *Stephen Garner*	33
Torn between Body and Soul: the Evolved Body in Theological Perspective *Nicola Hoggard Creegan*	55
Young People, Technoculture and Embodied Spirituality *Craig Mitchell*	73
List of Contributors	97

Editorial

Stephen Garner

Stephen Garner
School of Theology, University of Auckland, New Zealand

Several years ago a chain of fitness clubs in New Zealand ran an advertising campaign challenging people to sign up and 'be somebody'. The identification of body image with self worth is just one of many messages about the human body that we receive each day whether we're aware of them or not, and the slogan plays on the notion that all human beings are 'some body' regardless of what fitness programme they might choose to participate in. Indeed, embodiment is the primary lens through which all human beings view and encounter the world around them. As such, theological reflection upon the subject of the human body intersects with all manner of things that fall within human beings' lived experience.

The sheer breadth of this embodied engagement with life means that it is impossible to talk about a single theology of the body. One has only to look back through the history of the Christian tradition to find a plethora of competing interpretations related to the human body. Some theologies affirmed the human body as something good, while others took more negative views of the body seeing it as something to be marginalised or escaped from. Other theologies compete with different interpretations of the relationships between body and soul; body and mind; male and female; the eschatological destinies for the human body; race and culture; sexuality; marriage and family; birth and death; and how human beings bear the image and likeness of God. Significantly, theologies of the human body intersect with Christological ruminations on the exact nature of Jesus Christ's humanity, seen particularly in contending conceptions of the incarnation, the resurrection and salvation.

These historical reflections have also carried on into contemporary theological discussions about sexuality, gender, commercialisation and objectification of the body within various forms of media and advertising, disability, cosmetic or aesthetic surgery, medical and biotechnological developments, scientific descriptions of the human being, the role of the social sciences, and the nature of mediated communication. The human body itself serves as both a metaphorical and literal canvas for the exploration of what it means to be human beings in relationship with each other, with the wider world, and with God. Feminist theological critiques have highlighted how portrayals of the human body, and of sexuality and gender are caught up in complicated, and often oppressive, hierarchies of power between male and female in a variety of contexts and communities. Similarly, liberation theologians have explored how dominant notions of the human body have shaped political and economic landscapes, while the voices of indigenous theologians point to the need to reclaim local framings of the human body lost in the impact of colonisation.

Adam Cooper's introduction to the late Pope John Paul II's reflections on a theology of the body provides a useful starting point for this collection of essays. These reflections comprise a five-year series of catechetical lectures that aimed to develop an 'evangelical, Christian pedagogy of the body'. Taking Scripture, rather than physiology and psychology, as its starting point it constructs a threefold framework of original 'solitude', original 'unity' and original 'nakedness' that can then be used to interpret themes and questions relating to things such as human physicality, sexuality, marriage, procreation and contraception. Cooper's essay shows how this framework relates the uniqueness of the embodied human being within the creation, the universality of all human beings being bearers of God's image within their diversity, and the vulnerability found in the encounter with others to insights into an Incarnation that points to the salvation and redemption of embodied human beings and also to wisdom to live as embodied human beings. Cooper rightly notes that this serves as an example of 'a' theology of the body, rather than 'the' definitive theology, and as such it stands in dialogue with other interpretations within Catholicism and outside of that tradition.

Moving from a discussion related to Scripture serving as the primary source for engaging with the body theologically, Nicola Hoggard Creegan approaches her reflection upon the evolved embodied human being from the perspective of a dialogue between science and theology. Introducing her topic with Reinhold Niebuhr's paradoxical ambivalence of a humanity that is continually wrestling with its finitude and capacity for self-transcendence, she argues that characteristics that people might consider transcendent, such as the soul, or intelligence, or rationality emerge within an evolutionary process. This process places embodied human beings in the natural world, where we are part of the animal kingdom, yet also possessing the capacity to speak of the spiritual. This ability to bridge two worlds allows human beings to explore the concepts of dominion in and over creation in a way that guides ethical insight into wise living. In particular, Hoggard Creegan stresses that human knowing is linked inevitably to other forms of knowing through the body which are shared by others within the animal kingdom, and that this then opens up the possibility for the biblical mandate to dominion being made a relationship of mutual dependency and appreciation. The Incarnation again makes an appearance in this essay, highlighting the love of God for the whole embodied world and being linked to ethical behaviour.

While the most obvious connections between theology and body are commonly seen in terms of incarnation, sexuality and gender, Craig Mitchell highlights the subjects of age and mediated communication as related topics for discussion. In particular, Mitchell picks up on the tension introduced by new technologies and media that challenge traditional perceptions of embodied spirituality in young people. He argues that young persons' innate desires for intimacy and self-transcendence are bound up in their daily use of technology, leading to spiritual yearnings and practices that become 'embodied' in personal media practices. This challenges religious and theological commentaries on the bodily wellbeing of young people because those, he insists, have traditionally been connected to perceptions of sexuality as the lens through which adolescent development is measured. The promises and perils offered by mediating technology mirrors some similar concerns about adolescent development through that lens, and may in fact subsume adolescent sexuality. He concludes with the challenge that:

If young people seek and find spiritual experiences through mediated self-transcendence, then it is critical that churches and their youth ministries investigate whether this requires a shift from the view that authenticity in relationships is limited to physical presence or real-time communication.

We noted earlier that one of the areas where theology and the body were being explored was in the recovery of local accounts of the human body in a post colonial context by indigenous theologians. Parallel to this is the work offered here by Joanna Cruickshank, exploring historically the way in which perceptions of the human body amongst Moravian missionaries working in 19th century Australia shaped their form of Christian mission and also served as criteria for evaluating the effectiveness of that mission. She notes that across missionary communities the body served as marker of both conversion and the movement from 'savage' to civilised, capturing the notion that there is no 'gospel' free of culture. In her analysis of missionary-authored texts, Cruickshank examines how the theological heritage of Moravian missionaries from mid-nineteenth to early twentieth century interacted with reference to Aboriginal corporeality. In particular, the connections between the Moravian emphasis on the blood of Christ and sacrifice connected with the reverence for blood as sacred and powerful in many Aboriginal spiritual traditions provided avenues for dialogue and evangelism. Moreover, the way in which people comported themselves bodily after conversion served as a measure of the degree to which the Christian life had been embraced. Cruickshank highlights that this kind of approach was more complex that just looking to middle-class respectability, and that the Moravian missionary endeavour incorporated wide range of assumptions about human nature and progress. At times this meant significantly counter-cultural attitudes to the wider settler society in defending Aboriginal humanity, and at other times more narrow cultural perspectives that clashed with indigenous understandings of the body as a site of emotional expression.

Shifting from the nineteenth century to the twenty-first century, Stephen Garner argues that human technological agency generates anxieties concerning traditional concepts of the human body and the wider natural world. In particular, boundaries between organic and inorganic; human and machine; male and female are seen to shift and blur under the pressure of technological development. In this world, the figure of the 'cyborg'—the 'cybernetic organism'—becomes an increasingly common metaphor used to describe bodies being colonised by technology. These tensions generate what might be called 'narratives of apprehension' about human technological proclivity: on one hand there is anxiety about the potential of technology to do harm or to dehumanise, while on the other there is a simultaneous awe at the kinds of things that technology might achieve in improving the human condition. In his essay, Garner looks at what resources might be found within the Christian tradition to engage with the figure of the 'cyborg', arguing that contemporary explorations of a functional understanding of the doctrine of the image of God and human beings as 'created co-creators' are helpful here. That theological perspective combined with a vision of the embodied human being interconnected and interdependent with the wider natural world, and coupled with notions of social justice and the call to somehow exercise dominion wisely and justly, can open avenues, he argues, for wise living as 'image-bearing cyborgs'.

Each of the essays in this collection picks up the theme of embodiment as the lens through which they look at issues of theology and body, highlighting a rich vein to be mined in this area. As noted earlier though, reflection on the human body and theology is connected with the lived experience of individuals and communities, and as such, represents a broad and diverse field of study. These essays provide an engaging window onto this field, recognising though that there many further conversations to be had around the theme of the body and theology.

A Theology of the Body: Pope John Paul II's Catechetical Lectures

Adam G Cooper

Adam G Cooper
John Paul II Institute for Marriage and Family, Melbourne, Australia

This essay provides a basic introduction to the theology of the body of the late Pope John Paul II. John Paul II developed this lengthy theological work over the course of a five-year series of catechetical lectures given in Rome from September 1979 to November 1984. The lectures were addressed to the large weekly gatherings of pilgrims assembled at the Vatican on Wednesdays for prayer, catechesis, and the blessing of their universal pastor. Acclaimed or criticised, the collated and published versions of the lectures have captured worldwide attention.[1]

Catholic biblical scholar Luke Timothy Johnson has found the content too abstract.[2] Orthodox theologian David B. Hart perceives differently, instead describing it as enunciating 'with extraordinary fullness a complete vision of the spiritual and corporeal life of the human being; that vision is

---

1. There have been numerous English editions. For this essay I follow the recent translation by Michael Waldstein, based on a thorough critical evaluation of the original texts, entitled *Man and Woman He Created Them: A Theology of the Body* (Boston: Pauline Books, 2006).
2. Luke Timothy Johnson, 'A Disembodied 'Theology of the Body': John Paul II on Love, Sex, and Pleasure', Commonweal 128/2 (2001): 11–17. See also the response to Johnson by Christopher West, 'A Response to Luke Timothy Johnson's Critique of John Paul II's 'Disembodied' Theology of the Body', http://www.theologyofthebody.com/page.asp?ContentID=75, accessed March 30, 2009.

a self-sufficient totality, which one is free to embrace or reject as a whole.'[3] Lutheran Robert Jenson offers more reserved praise, first noting the limits of the catechesis, which 'does not present what the title might suggest, a systematic locus *de corpore hominis*', but then defending its essential relevance with the assertion that the catecheses themselves are 'not exercises in casuistry, but are rather specifically theological and indeed pastoral. They trace the "*revelation*" of the body, from discovery by "the man" of his own body, in the beginning, through the perverted but still wonderful experience of "historical man" with his body, to the body's final glorification in God.'[4] Jenson's former observation of course accords with the Pope's speculative, sometimes even hesitant tone and numerous suggestive excurses. Clearly he never meant it to be the last word on the subject but a catalyst for further reflection.

Jenson's second point is worth highlighting too. If it is not *the* definitive theology of the body, as the new English subtitle to the lectures properly qualifies, John Paul II's theology of the body is precisely a *theology* and not a physiology, psychology, philosophy or even a phenomenology. Theology, at least according to the traditional meaning of the word, studies things first of all as they stand in relation to God. Theology tries to adopt God's perspective on things, to learn what God has to say about them. Of course, as a human activity, theology draws deeply upon the vast range of human experience and reason; it listens carefully to what can be known about things through other disciplines and avenues of learning. Ultimately however, theology—as someone like Origen or Dionysius the Areopagite or even Thomas Aquinas would have said—finds its authoritative basis and reference point in God's own word.

Thus it is no surprise to find that the theology of the body is basically a big bible study. Moreover, it is a bible study with a distinctly practical aim. According to John Paul II, the contents of the catechesis are not just a theory, but rather an 'evangelical, Christian pedagogy of the body.' He goes on: 'This pedagogic character comes from the character of the Bible and above all of the Gospel as a salvific message revealing *what man's true*

---

3. David B Hart, 'The Anti-Theology of the Body', *The New Atlantis* (Summer, 2005), http://www.thenewatlantis.com/publications/the-anti-theology-of-the-body, accessed March 30, 2009.
4. Robert W Jenson, 'Reading the Body', *The New Atlantis* (Summer, 2005), http://www.thenewatlantis.com/publications/reading-the-body, accessed March 30, 2009.

good is for the sake of shaping—according to the measure of this good—his life on earth in the perspective of the hope of the future world.'[5] The main title of the revised translation, 'Man and Woman He Created Them', taken from the biblical account of creation in Genesis 1, serve as a kind of *leitmotiv* for the whole study. For it was John Paul II's conviction that the human body, precisely in its sexed duality, has been created specifically 'to transfer into the visible reality of the world the mystery hidden from eternity in God, and to be a sign of it.'[6] What we read in the Genesis narrative not only echoes some of the deepest intuitions and anxieties of human experience, but manifests a gratuitous, divine trajectory.

As far as methodology goes, the entire study constituted by the lectures proceeds by way of a careful, meditative reading of certain central biblical passages that deal with marriage, sexuality, and our bodily life. Although there is something of what we might recognise as a critical exegesis of the original texts, it is clear that the Pope's exegetical method bears its own unique stamp. Not without scientific and historical rigour, it is at the same time contemplative and creative, moral and mystical, almost in keeping with more traditional modes of Christian engagement with Scripture. It is true, as the Pope explicitly acknowledges, that a far-reaching biblical study on the theology of the body would have to touch on matters much wider than sexuality, such as human suffering and death. His focus, however, is inspired by the fact that the redemption of the body has been brought about by a covenantal act on God's part that is at once sacrificial and spousal in character. It is for a special sort of marriage that God first created humanity. It is by a special sort of marriage that God has redeemed it.

The first half of the study, in three sections, is largely based on the teaching of Jesus in the Gospels. The Pope attends to certain 'key words' of Jesus, so-called because they unlock, as it were, the meaning of human physicality. The second half, also in three sections, is based on passages drawn more widely from Saint Paul and from the Old Testament's Song of Songs and the lesser known Book of Tobit. All along, John Paul II draws in reflections from all over Scripture—not to mention the writings of the church fathers, the church's sacramental practices, and insights from art, philosophy and psychology. He also applies these insights to numerous

---

5. *Man and Woman He Created Them: A Theology of the Body* [hereon TOB], catechesis 122, paragraph 5 [=122.5].
6. TOB 19.4.

moral questions relating to the sexuality and marriage, including celibacy, pornography, procreation, and contraception. Of note is the fact that the study ends with a careful re-reading of Pope Paul VI's controversial 1968 encyclical, *Humanae Vitae*, on which John Paul II's theology of the body may be taken as an extensive theological commentary. Indeed, as he acknowledges, the very sharpness of the reaction stirred up by *Humanae Vitae* 'confirms the importance and difficulty of these questions.'[7]

The Occasion for the Theology of the Body

The decision to embark upon a sustained study of marriage, sexuality and bodily life was no doubt occasioned by numerous factors, not least of all the Pope's own personal penchant for the subject. From his early days as a graduate student in philosophy, particularly of the phenomenological school, Karol Wojtyla exhibited the marked influence of what has been called the 'corporeal turn' in philosophy, with its renewed interest in the physical and concrete.[8] Important as this background factor is, however, I would like to suggest four more proximate and, somehow, more simple reasons.

First of all, in his office as universal pontiff, John Paul II was simply taking up a long-standing fundamental locus of incarnational and sacramental theology. The whole religion of Christianity is centred around the person of Jesus of Nazareth, who was and is a bodily, sexual being. But this Jesus, says Christianity, docile to the apostolic witness, is also somehow divine. This real man, with a real body, is none other than God himself in the world, God living among us as a flesh and blood human being. Christianity is the religion whose focus of faith and worship is this God-man Jesus, whom the first Christians knew as God's enfleshed Word or Logos. So it shouldn't surprise us that the body is an object of great inter-

---

7. TOB 133.2.
8. See Kenneth L Schmitz, *At the Center of the Human Drama: The Philosophical Anthropology of Karol Wojtyla/Pope John Paul II* (Washington DC: The Catholic University of America Press, 1993); Jaroslaw Kupczak, *Destined for Liberty: The Human Person in the Philosophy of Karol Wojtyla/John Paul II* (Washington DC: Catholic University of America Press, 2000). Schmitz refers to Wojtyla's 'new sense of the concrete' (140). On the ever increasing use of the term 'the corporeal turn', see Maxine Sheets-Johnstone (ed), *The Corporeal Turn: An Interdisciplinary Reader* (Exeter, UK: Imprint Academic, 2009).

est for Christian theology. In the famous explanation of Pope John Paul II, 'Through the fact that the Word of God became flesh, the body entered theology . . . through the [front] door.'[9] In short, Jesus is God's theology (*theo-logia*) of the body in person.

Second, in his teaching, John Paul II is attentive to the fact that in the Gospels Jesus himself specifically addresses such topics as sexuality and morality and marriage, and does so with special reference to the Creator's original plan for men and women from the beginning. The disciples of Christ cannot but consider in faith his teaching on these issues. Being a Christian does not simply mean giving mental assent to certain ideas, but involves surrender to a calling or vocation in which we participate in Christ's active retrieval of the original dignity of the sexed human body.

Third, while the Christian Church has always taught frankly on matters of marriage and sexuality, it has not always offered a winsome and positive rationale for its teaching. John Paul II, who from his early experience as a priest had a heart for the spiritual wellbeing of the young and was closely involved in preparing many couples for marriage, wanted to show how the traditional teaching of the Catholic Church on moral issues makes good sense, given the kind of bodily beings we are and the kinds of desires we have for pleasure, fulfilment, faithfulness, and love. Knowing how Catholic moral teaching had been experienced by many people as legalistic, burdensome, or simply irrational, he wanted to explore the ways it corresponds to the intrinsic truth of our psychophysical constitution.

The fourth and final reason I'd like to suggest as one that offered an occasion for the Pope's theology of the body is the tidal wave of sexual insanity that has flooded our contemporary world, and began doing so at least from the 1960s, though probably before. It is no exaggeration to say that people today, like never before, are obsessed with sex and the body. One need only think, for example, of our primary western cultural forms: music, media, movies. With few exceptions, they appear saturated with more or less explicit pornographic and exploitative themes. The problem with these themes, as John Paul II would argue, does not lie in the fact that they are sexual. The problem lies rather in the perverse and abusive ways they present sexuality. One may think also about the sports and fashion and cosmetic industries, and the way they feed and respond to our anxiet-

---

9. *TOB* 23.4.

ies about the body, its health, its appearance. Like no other era in history, it seems, the sexualised body has been idolised as a god. Of course, the ancient world had its sexual vices too. But in our time, the ancient connection between sex and the fecundity or fruitfulness of nature, has been totally severed: love is not allowed to be fruitful. The perennial problem here is ultimately simple: when you divinise sex, you destroy it; when you satiate desire, you strangle it. In the words of the well-known feminist author Naomi Wolf, 'The onslaught of porn is responsible for deadening male libido in relation to real women . . . [S]exual appetite has become like the relationship between agribusiness, processed foods, supersize portions, and obesity . . . If your appetite is stimulated and fed by poor-quality material, it takes more junk to fill you up.'[10] Western societies have reached the point where people habitually turn to technology and technique to try and create for themselves what in the end can only be received as a gift and cultivated through self-sacrifice: personal communion. With this confused culture in mind, the Pope's teaching on sex and the body can be taken as an attempt to reveal that we are more than our sexuality, that our body, with all its anxieties, yearnings and vulnerabilities, represents a physical-spiritual whole, a personal being created to reflect God's own beauty and to discover true joy in giving and receiving fruitful love.

Back to the Beginning

I stated above that the theology of the body is basically a big bible study in six parts, the first three of which are devoted to an elaboration of certain key words of Jesus. The first part actually begins by following Jesus' lead in going back to 'the beginning' (Matt 19:8), to learn from God's perspective what sex and the body and marriage are all about. At one level 'the beginning' refers to the beginning of the Bible, where we find the account of God's creation of man and woman. But at another level, according to John Paul II, the 'beginning' signifies something much deeper. When Jesus refers his hearers back to the beginning, he is referring them to 'the first inheritance of every human being in the world', 'the first witness of human identity according to the word of God', 'the first source of the certainty of

---

10. Quoted by Mary Eberstadt, 'The Vindication of *Humanae Vitae*', *First Things* 185 (August/September 2008): 39.

our vocation as persons created in God's image.' In other words, these 'beginning' chapters of Genesis are not meant to be read like a scientific text or history book, but are to be engaged as a kind of power-packed dramatic script, composed by God, depicting the defining structures and relationships that underlie human life in the universe.

When we return to the beginning this way, says John Paul, we discover three original or primal experiences that characterise the 'state of original innocence', that is, the dynamic vocation God originally planned for us but from which human beings have subsequently become estranged through sin. These three primal experiences serve as kind of interpretive key to understanding all that follows in the theology of the body. They lie at the very boundary of our historic human experience, and so they lie somehow beyond us, inaccessible to us. Yet by appealing to this beginning, Jesus was not just setting us up with an ideal which can never be realised. Rather, as the Saviour and Redeemer and Lover of humanity, he has invited all people to learn from him how it is possible to retrieve this original dignity, to discover how, through the redemption of our bodies which he effectively realised on the cross, he has opened up the way for these original experiences to be ours, just as God planned. The three experiences which characterise this state of innocence are: (1) original solitude; (2) original unity; and (3) original nakedness. I shall here try to paraphrase the Pope's sometimes complex and circular meditations on these three themes, adopting a certain directness perhaps more apposite to the catechetical genre.[11]

Original Solitude

The first 'original' experience suggested by John Paul is that of solitude. Of all the thousands of species of living animals that populate planet earth, human beings stand out as unique. It is true, we are animals: complex organic, sensate beings, adapted to our environment, with deep instincts for survival. This is the most basic thing about us. But we know we are more than animals. Animals don't compose operas. Animals don't explore outer or inner space. We are animals, but we are wonderful, wondering animals—animals with a difference. We can think, ask questions, give rea-

---

11. I have benefited in this approach from Tony Percy, *Theology of the Body Made Simple* (Ballan, Australia: Connor Court, 2005), 13–34.

sons, wonder why or why not, love, forgive, hope. Yet with a little reflection, we realise that there's no reason why we *have* to exist, either individually, or as a species. Something or someone, it seems, wanted us here. That someone is God. We are created by God, we are created for God in such a way that our meaning and fulfilment rests with God.

That is how it was in the Genesis story, as John Paul reads it. God places the man in the Paradise he has prepared for him, to make his life there and to honour God with his work and worship. But somehow being alone with God is not everything. 'It is not good for the man to be alone' (Gen 2: 18). We are not made for solitary existence, just 'God and me and no one else.' We are also social beings. We need fellow beings like ourselves to become ourselves, to reach our proper maturity. Our sense of isolation when we consider our aloneness in the universe reveals our dependence, our need for relation, for fellowship, for communion: with God, first of all, but also with our fellow creatures, though not just any fellow creatures, but ones that know us and understand us and are like us. 'It is not good for the man to be alone', says the Creator, so God sets out to make a partner to complement the man, someone the same, but someone different.

Original Unity

The second original experience is unity. For all their amazing diversity, human beings share in common a fundamental unity and solidarity. They all bear God's image, some profound trace of his presence and activity and purpose. Yet casting our eye around, paying attention to the bodies God has given us, we notice how we are nonetheless different. Acknowledging the occasional presence of genetic anomalies, by and large half of us are males, half of us are females, terms which imply correlation or intelligibility only in terms of the other. Original solitude tells us that we are bodily. Original unity tells us that there are two different ways we are bodily. The differences appear more than physical. We think differently. We behave differently. In some cases the differences become polar. Yet when man and woman couple, an event as moral and spiritual as it is physical, it is like they are made for each other. Their bodies are spousally designed, nuptially ordered: they fit together hand in glove. The deep attraction between the sexes, an attraction analogous to their physical complementarity, is native to the human species; it cannot be effaced. Were it to be lost, the survival of the race would be lost with it, for with the attraction goes the power to procreate.

And so, at the beginning, the woman, creatively constructed by God from Adam's own body, elicits from the man an exclamation of joyful discovery. In the first words ever uttered by a human being, he calls her 'bone of my bone, flesh of my flesh.' He is overwhelmed by this new being in his life. She is not like the other animals; she is some-one, just like him. Yet, as anyone can tell, she is not like him, but is very, very different. He recognises and receives her as someone else, someone created to face him, to complement him, to be his mutual counterpart. In one way, she answers to some deep-seated need in him for personal communion, which no non-human animal can satisfy. So profound is the union that these two discover in marital intercourse, that the Bible calls it a 'one flesh' union (Gen 2: 23). Yet though the man will abandon everything for her, she is not his property. She is a gift, reminding him that she does not replace their common, deeper need for God. Of course, these observations accept the patriarchal perspective of the Genesis narrative as normative, realising that other more critical readings, which question the right of a man to define a woman in terms of himself, are possible.

Original Nakedness

The third original experience is nakedness. Our experience of our own body teaches us that covering it up with clothing is more than just a way of keeping warm. For a child, tearing around naked is just plain good fun.[12] But as we grow we learn that it isn't safe to undress just anywhere, anytime. To be naked is to be vulnerable. Here we learn again that we are more than our bodies. On the one hand nakedness describes a physical state. But the vulnerability that accompanies it is much more than physical. We all know what we mean when we speak of our personal space, personal boundaries. Covering our naked bodies is a way of protecting our space, of guarding our boundaries from unwanted invasion. The shame we would feel were some stranger to catch us undressing is a good shame, a positive shame.

---

12. See Percy, *Theology of the Body Made Simple*, 28.

We feel it, because we instinctively don't want to be used. We don't want to be known in our vulnerability except by someone who we know will not use us in our vulnerability. Not to feel shame, when the conditions warrant it, is to be shameless. Shamelessness, the incapacity to feel shame, is what we descend to when, due to the degrading cycle of using and being used, all self-consciousness, all sense of dignity, all sense of modesty and discretion, has been lost. And when these are lost, so is self-mastery lost, the ability to give oneself, and to receive another, freely, voluntarily, as gift. By contrast, when in a wholesome marriage, for example, a couple embodies the one flesh communion of original unity, or when, before a fellow human being or before God, unconditional love and acceptance swallow up all fear of criticism and exploitation, then there can be physical nakedness, personal vulnerability, without shame.

Nuptial Symbolism

According to John Paul II's theology of the body, each of these three 'originals' belongs to the state of original innocence, a state that we wish we knew, but that we have left behind, a state that fallen humanity has lost. Standing between historical humanity and these three originals is another 'original', so-called 'original sin', which refers not so much to the sinful act of the first couple, but rather to the universal human state of being out of kilter with God, with each other, and with the cosmos. It is, to borrow Karl Barth's idea, a kind of 'presupposition' underlying our empirical experience. Our relationships with each other are too often marred by destructive impulses, many of which manifest various forms of lust: the lust for power, the lust for pleasure, the lust for glory. The external dignity of the body is threatened by the disorder of our interior motivations.

Yet there is something of these three 'originals' that lingers on, like a vague memory, in the fundamental yearnings we experience as simultaneously bodily and spiritual beings. Reflecting a celebrated Augustinian and Thomistic perception, John Paul knows that we are creatures of desire, and that this desire is necessary to inspire passionate, intentional, deliberate action. We are made to love. All we need, somehow, is for our loves to be directed towards the right objects, in the right way.

How do the three originals come to figure positively within our current mode of existence? 'Solitude' encapsulates that sense of the uniqueness of human beings in the universe, the realisation and awareness of our fundamental open-endedness, our orientation towards something more than ourselves and this universe. Solitude reminds us that we are not self-sufficient, that we have a deep inner yearning and need for more than we can ever give ourselves. The solitude of the human body among all other bodies symbolises that all is gift: that we are essentially creatures made to receive, that our bodily being is already a sign that we come from God, that as physical beings we manifest in the world at the level of the tangible and visible something which is mysteriously intangible and invisible.

'Unity' encapsulates that profound complementarity between the sexes, without which the race wouldn't exist, starting with the experience between men and women of physical sexual attraction and culminating in the fruitful, one flesh intimacy of marital union. Unity reminds us that the symbolism of the human body is a nuptial symbolism, which means not only that it is endowed with the fertile power to cooperate with God in the work of creation, but that it is also shaped for fulfilment in a communion of persons.

'Nakedness' encapsulates the yearning we experience to be free from all fearful constraints about our physical and personal vulnerability, to be free from exposure and exploitation, to be free to own ourselves as we are, and so be able to give ourselves not out of coercion or manipulation, but out of love. Nakedness reminds us that the human body, though fallen now, is properly God's good creation, pure and free to reveal the truth of who we are, to realise the truth of what God wants us to be.

Salvation as Gift

I have summarised in brief outline the foundational points only from the very first part of John Paul II's theology of the body. To the extent that his readers can grasp these three 'originals', they are well placed to understand all that the former Pope has to say in the rest of his catechesis on more 'practical' matters such as sin, sex, desire, pornography, marriage, celibacy, death, contraception, prayer, the sacraments, ascesis, and so on. To investigate the way John Paul II expounds these topics would take more space than we have here. However, it may be worth adding one or two closing remarks along those lines. If the first third of the theology of the body is the Pope's attempt to follow Jesus back to the beginning, to learn there what human beings should be, and what they should become, then to stop there is to leave off without any clear idea how to fulfil this calling. Indeed, some may wonder in reading these opening chapters whether there is enough account taken of the very real failures in the realm of bodily and sexual experience, of the very common experience of an incapacity, sometimes despite best intentions, to realise the full contours of our calling to personal communion with God and with one another. At root, these failings reveal that the human problem is not with sex or the body, even if sex and the body function as especially obvious zones in which these failings adopt a peculiar form with often disturbing effects. The malady rather lies deeper, in the heart. The heart is the centre of our being, and when the centre of our being goes wrong, everything else goes wrong too. Nor is it simply a matter of trying harder, or promising to do better next time. We really need a new or renewed heart, one somehow transfigured by grace.

John Paul II is not unaware of this tension, even if his treatment of it sometimes unfolds indirectly. It is precisely with the shadow of these deeper failings and incapacities in view that he tries to show how the gospel of Jesus Christ has meaning for contemporary persons. And this is surely the burden of his theology of the body: to outline a moral and spiritual pedagogy illumined by christological truth. For John Paul II, the Christ event is not simply a revelation of God. It is a revelation of humanity. When God the Son became flesh, he manifested the truth of human bodily life with all its limitations, all its vulnerabilities, all its temptations, all its possibilities. He did not live among his peers as an angel, immune to the multitude of physical and emotional and spiritual forces that pull human beings in different directions. But neither did he succumb to those forces, as we typically do, nor did he allow them to alienate his heart from God, from himself, and from his fellow human beings, not even from those who hated him. Inasmuch as Christ reveals the truth of what it means to be a person, his body—and the bodily life he lives among us - has become a place of healing, a place of recovery and restitution. One may recall George Herbert's beautiful lines:

> Christ hath took in this piece of ground,
> And made a garden there for those
> Who want herbs for their wound.[13]

Christianity holds that where Christ's body is, there is all of God. The Church teaches that in the man Jesus of Nazareth the fullness of divine life became physically present and permanently available in space and time. It believes that God's love for humanity is essentially ecstatic, such that he goes out of himself and actually becomes the object of his love, willingly suffering in his body the same kind of abuse, torture, and violent treatment that have plagued human history since the dawn of time. But it also believes that this love was not exhausted by his death, but that he physically rose from the state of death, overcoming the final barrier that borders personal human existence and threatens the species with final extinction. These are the basic lineaments of an incarnational theology. And if all that is true, then the truth is that even the human body, with all the sin and evil it has suffered or been involved in, can through the body of Jesus Christ be healed from evil, delivered from death, and united to God. For in his cross, Christ has not just exemplified loving with one's body, but has realised it, decisively fulfilled it, for the world. Christ speaks the language of love not just with words, but through the body-language of death and resurrection. And so now his body, which is encountered mysteriously in the communion of persons which constitutes his Church, has become for all who come to him in trust and hope the source and sign and sacrament of a new life, a fully physical life, but a fully holy life too, in which that original, nuptial meaning of our bodies, inscribed in a sort of blueprint at the beginning of creation, finds its proper fulfilment and goal in us. For John Paul II, the redemption of the body in Christ reveals not just an ethical truth, but an anthropological truth as well, or rather, *the* anthropological truth.[14] In fleshing this truth out in studied

---

13. George Herbert, 'Sunday' lines 40–42, in John N Wall (ed), *George Herbert: The Country Parson, The Temple* (New York: Paulist Press, 1981), 193.
14. TOB 58.5. Cf. Vatican II's *Pastoral Constitution on the Church in the Modern World* (*Gaudium et Spes*) and its famous passages habitually quoted by John Paul II (§22): 'The truth is that only in the mystery of the incarnate Word does the mystery of man take on light . . . Christ, the final Adam, by the revelation of the mystery of the Father and his love, fully reveals man to man himself and makes his supreme calling clear' (Homebush, NSW: Society of Saint Paul, 1978), 31.

dialogue with the Church's scriptures and tradition, John Paul II has done two things. He has joined redemption with creation, salvation with ethics, bringing together again two spheres that the perennial spirit of gnosticism will always try to keep apart. And he has spoken the gospel with peculiar profundity and clarity, enabling salvation in Christ to be encountered in a new way—and perhaps for many of his readers, even for the first time—as sheer and total gift.

Blood, Tears and Race:
Moravian Missionaries and Indigenous Bodies in Colonial Australia

Joanna Cruickshank

Joanna Cruickshank
School of History Heritage and Society, Deakin University, Victoria, Australia

In 1866, a German Moravian missionary named CW Kramer, working at the Aboriginal mission of Ramahyuck in rural Victoria, wrote a report on the progress he believed was being made at the mission. Describing two candidates for baptism, he noted:

> What a difference there is between even the looks of these two young men and those of the heathen! As they saw the church-building advancing and the day of their baptism drawing nearer and nearer, their faces beamed with joy, and they went about constantly singing hymns.[1]

This description suggested that the distinction between Christian and 'heathen' could be recognised in the 'looks' or bodily appearance of Aboriginal people. Such a perceptible difference provided welcome evidence to the missionary and to his audience of missionary supporters, of the effectiveness of the Christian missionary effort.

Kramer's comments about the difference between the 'looks' of Christian and 'heathen' Aboriginal people supports recent work by a number

---

1. CW Kramer, Report on Ramahyuck, *Periodical Accounts Relating to the Missions of the Church of the United Brethren, Established Among the Heathen*, 26 (1866): 32.

of historians, who have noted that missionaries operating in the colonial context paid close attention to the bodies of the Indigenous people they evangelised. This concern with Indigenous corporeality has generally been seen within a postcolonial framework, in which missions are understood primarily as an aspect of European colonising. For example, in his study of Methodist missionaries in early twentieth-century Papua and New Guinea, Richard Eves argues that the missionaries attempted to 'refashion' the bodies of Pacific Islanders into appearances, practices and gestures that demonstrated the presence of 'disciplined' Christian character as it was understood in Britain. These behaviours were defined in opposition to the 'natural' state of the Islanders. 'In this context,' Eves argues, 'the disciplined body acts as a marker both of conversion and of the move from "savage" to "civilised".'[2] Similarly, in his study of the Ramahyuck mission where Kramer worked, Bain Attwood claims that missionaries used the spatial structures of the mission as well as their teaching to engender new understandings of the body and bodily practices among Aboriginal residents.[3] Attwood interprets this as part of the missionaries' broader project to remake Aboriginal people in their own image, which involved both 'Christianising' and 'civilising' them in accordance with nineteenth-century missionary theory.[4] Such interpretations clearly draw heavily on Foucault in seeing the body 'primarily as a site of subjugation and dominance'.[5]

This approach has been productive in teasing out the complicated relationship between missions and colonialism and also in understanding the disruptive impact of missionary activity, particularly residential missions, on Indigenous communities and their cultures. It is, however, limited on a number of counts. In the first place, as Jacqueline van Gent notes, it does not engage in any significant way with Indigenous perceptions of the body, which could, as in the case of the Western Arrernte people she examines, emphasise 'a person's spiritual and somatic interdependence

---

2. Richard Eves, 'Colonialism, Corporeality and Character: Methodist Missions and the Refashioning of Bodies in the Pacific', in *History and Anthropology* 10/1 (1996): 86.
3. Bain Attwood, *The Making of the Aborigines* (Sydney: Allen & Unwin, 1989), 20–21.
4. Attwood, *The Making of the Aborigines*, 1–2.
5. Jacqueline van Gent, 'Changing Concepts of Embodiment and Illness among the Western Arrernte at Hermansburg Mission', in *Journal of Religious History* 27/3 (2003): 329.

with kin and ancestors'.⁶ As her study shows, the body could become a site of connection, negotiation and resistance as well as control. Secondly, historians adopting this approach to missionary attitudes and practices rarely pay attention to the theological aspects of missionary practice. Missionaries are understood within the history of colonialism, or the history of European thought, rather than within the history of Christianity and the specifics of their own denominational theology.⁷ While this focus is an understandable reaction to the long tradition of hagiographical mission histories produced for denominational purposes, it is problematic in fully understanding missionary practices and their consequences.

In this article, therefore, I begin by considering the theological heritage of the Moravian missionaries who worked in Australia from the mid-nineteenth to the early twentieth century. I examine how this heritage helps illuminate the ways in which they made references to Aboriginal corporeality in their writings, specifically in relation to bodily displays of emotion. It is important to note that this article does not claim to represent an Indigenous perspective on missions, as it is primarily an analysis of missionary-authored texts. While such an account risks simply adding to the already one-sided scholarly history of missions, my hope is that a more nuanced understanding of missionaries will contribute to the task of understanding the impact of missions for Indigenous people in Australia and elsewhere.

Moravians

The Moravian missionaries who worked in Australia were part of one of the oldest missionary traditions within Protestantism. The Moravian movement, (also known as the *Unitas Fratrum* or *Brüdergemeine* or *Brüder-Unität*), traced its heritage to the followers of fifteenth-century proto-Reformer Jan Hus. Fleeing Roman Catholic persecution in the 1720s, the remnant of the Moravian community found its way to Upper Lusatia in Saxony, where they were allowed to settle on Bethelsdorf, the

---

6. Ibid.
7. For example, Eves relies for his understanding of Methodism on a few highly-contested twentieth-century interpretations of Methodism such as EP Thompson's *The Making of the English Working Class* (London: Penguin Books, 1991).

country estate of Count Nicolaus Ludwig von Zinzendorf.⁸ Zinzendorf, who had studied under August Hermann Franke at Halle, was a convinced Pietist and an enthusiastic believer in the establishment of Christian communities that could live out Pietist principles. The Moravians joined a diverse group of Protestant refugees who had already been given shelter on Zinzendorf's estates and in 1727 Zinzendorf moved permanently to Bethelsdorf to lead the community.⁹ He issued two sets of 'Statutes' for the community, which outlined the principles and rules by which he believed the group could live in love and humility, 'maintain the pure evangelical doctrine, simplicity and grace' and seek the conversion of souls.¹⁰

From the early days of their revitalisation under Zinzendorf, who had been influenced by the missionary concerns of Halle Pietism, the Moravians adopted a missionary outlook. In 1732, Moravian Brethren went as missionaries to the Danish West Indies. Sixty years later, there were Moravian missionaries in twenty-seven different locations around the world.¹¹ By the nineteenth century the Moravians were famous as missionary pioneers and examplars, willing to work in places and among people at whom their less zealous or hardy evangelical brethren baulked. It was not surprising, therefore, that by the nineteenth century they were receiving invitations from the Australian colonies to come and work among the Indigenous peoples of these colonies. The devastation that colonisation had wrought among Aboriginal communities was obvious, settlers were generally more interested in dispossessing Indigenous people than establishing missions among them, and those mission ventures that had been

---

8. Robert Kenny, *The Lamb Enters the Dreaming: Nathanael Pepper & the Ruptured World* (Melbourne: Scribe, 2007), 7–9.
9. Peter Vogt, 'Nicholas Ludwig von Zinzendorf (1700-1760)' in *The Pietist Theologians: An Introduction to Theology in the Seventeenth and Eighteenth Centuries*, edited by Carter Lindberg (Malden, MA: Blackwell, 2005), 208–209.
10. Nicolas Ludwig, Count von Zinzendorf 'Brotherly Union and Agreement at Herrnhut' (1727), in *Pietists: Selected Writings*, edited by Peter C Erb (London: SPCK, 1983), 325–329.
11. For an overview of the early missionary efforts of the Moravians, see Felicity Jensz, 'Collecting Cultures for God: German Moravian Missionaries and the British Colony of Victoria, Australia, 1848-1908' (PhD Thesis, University of Melbourne, 2007), 35–39.

attempted among Aboriginal people were largely regarded as unsuccessful.[12]

In 1850, therefore a small team of Moravian brethren made a first attempt to establish a mission in rural Victoria. Though ultimately abortive, this was the beginning of an enduring Moravian missionary presence in Australia. In 1858, two young Moravians, Friedrich Hagenauer and Friedrich Spieseke, arrived in Victoria and established the Ebenezer mission in the Wimmera. Four years later, Hagenauer moved to Gippsland and established Ramahyuck mission. These Victorian missions were followed by others (mostly short-lived) in South Australia and, in the late nineteenth and early twentieth centuries, by a series of missions in Far North Queensland, including Mapoon, Aurukun and Weipa.[13] The Victorian and Queensland missions were largely funded by the Presbyterian churches of these colonies/states, and the Moravian missionaries were employed by them. The last Moravian missionaries working in Australia retired in 1919.

Blood

In 1755, Zinzendorf defended the Moravian Brethren to a suspicious English public, in a lengthy 'Exposition', published in the context of controversies over Moravian theology and practices. Among a number of accusations which he noted had been made against the Brethren and against his own teaching, two in particular are noteworthy. Firstly, the Moravians had been 'distinguished for their using the Words Blood, Lamb and Wounds.' Zinzendorf indignantly defended the orthodoxy of Moravian practice in this regard, appealing 'to the Privy Council of Dresden, and to

---

12. For a good brief overview of the challenges faced by missionaries in colonial Australia, see Patricia Grimshaw, 'Missions, Colonialism and the Politics of Gender' in *Evangelists of Empire? Missionaries in Colonial History*, edited by Amanda Barry, Joanna Cruickshank, Andrew May and Patricia Grimshaw (Melbourne: School of Historical Studies and eScholarship Research Centre, 2008), 6–7. Also online at http://msp.esrc.unimelb.edu.au/shs/missions.

13. For an account of the establishment of the North Queensland missions, including Hagenauer's significant role in this process, see Joanna Cruickshank and Patricia Grimshaw, 'A Matter of No Small Importance to the Colony': Moravian Missionaries on Cape York Peninsula, Queensland, 1891–1919' in *Missionaries, Indigenous Peoples and Cultural Exchange*, edited by Patricia Grimshaw and Andrew May (Sussex Academic Press, 2009).

all Mankind, whether fifty Years ago such an Accusation would have been endured among Lutherans?'[14] A second accusation, made more directly against Zinzendorf, was 'That he teaches, according to our Saviour's Declaration, *No Man knoweth the Father save the Son, and he to whomsoever the Son will reveal Him*. And again, *No Man cometh unto the Father but by Me*. Matt. xi. 27. John xiv. 6.' The consequence of this Christological emphasis was that Zinzendorf argued that 'Divines do wrong, who presume to *begin their System with the Father*.'[15] Zinzendorf defended these aspects of Moravian practice—the devotional language of sacrifice and suffering and the primacy of Christ in revelation—as orthodox. Nonetheless, each of these elements was distinctively (and enduringly) Moravian, and evidence of a particularly Christocentric theology.

Zinzendorf followed Luther in seeing the atoning death of Christ as the objective grounds for the justification and sanctification of sinful human beings. Sinners could not earn salvation, but only rest in child-like trust on the saving work of Christ. Righteousness was always imputed, never inherent. For Zinzendorf, this 'theology of the cross' led to a radical Christocentrism.[16] 'The concept that distinguishes what is Christian from all other concepts, societies, and states of mind,' Zinzendorf contended, 'is the doctrine of the sacrificial blood of the Creator, poured out for us in order to redeem us from sin'.[17] As this statement demonstrates, for Zinzendorf, the God of whom Scripture spoke was everywhere the Son. The titles of 'Creator', 'Jehovah' and even 'Father' could rightly be applied to Christ.[18] It was for this reason that Zinzendorf believed that doctrinal systems, and Christian preaching, must begin with Christ crucified.

From his Pietist background, Zinzendorf retained a strong emphasis on 'heart-religion' (*Herzenreligion*), teaching that as reason could never accept the belief that God was the crucified Jesus, faith must come through

---

14. These quotes are from English Moravian John Hutton's summary of Zinzendorf's response in the introduction to Nicholaus von Zinzendorf, *An Exposition, or True State, of the Matters objected in England to the People known by the Name of Unitas Fratrum*, edited by John Hutton (London, 1755), v.
15. Zinzendorf, *An Exposition*, vi.
16. Vogt, 'Nicholas Ludwig von Zinzendorf', 211.
17. Zinzendorf, 'Homilies on the Litany of Wounds' (1742), quoted in Vogt, 'Nicholas Ludwig von Zinzendorf', 212.
18. Vogt, 'Nicholas Ludwig von Zinzendorf', 211.

a transformative experience of the suffering Jesus.[19] 'The Savior has to appear before a human soul', he preached, 'she has to come to know him in his bloody wounds, his martyred person must stand for her before the inner eye, her imagination must be filled with him'.[20] Unlike some Pietist theologians, Zinzendorf did not believe that conversion must be preceded by a lengthy and intense period of distress.[21] Conversion was nonetheless an emotional experience, in which pity for Christ's sacrificial suffering produced grief at one's own sinfulness, which was replaced by a faith that was experienced as inner assurance. 'Heart-religion' was not simply a matter of conversion, however, but of a life lived moment-by-moment in felt reliance on Christ. A constant focus on the crucified Jesus produced ongoing faith and personal change.

This combination of a Lutheran focus on the atoning death of Christ and a Pietist experientialism produced, as criticisms of the Moravians suggested, an unusually intense devotion to the physical sufferings of Jesus. 'Blood' became the key term for referring to Christ's sacrifice.[22] Famously, however, Moravian devotion focused not only on the blood of Jesus, but also on his wounds, which were imagined as a source of comfort and refuge for the sinner. In the 1740s, Zinzendorf composed a 'Litany of the Wounds of the Husband,' which took this tendency to an extreme.

> Woundrous wounds of Jesus, *Holy fissures, you make sinners holy, and thieves from saints. How amazing!*
> Powerful wounds of Jesus, *So moist, so gory, bleed on my heart so that I may remain brave and like the wound . . .*
> Juicy wounds of Jesus, *Whoever sharpens the pen and with it pierces you just a little, licks and tastes it.*[23]

---

19. Vogt, 'Nicholas Ludwig von Zinzendorf', 213.
20. Zinzendorf, *Londoner Reden I*, quoted in Vogt, 'Nicholas Ludwig von Zinzendorf', 213.
21. Bruce Hindmarsh discusses Zinzendorf's understanding of the conversion process in *The Evangelical Conversion Narrative: Spiritual Autobiography in Early Modern England* (Oxford: Oxford University Press, 2005), 164–165.
22. Benjamin A Pugh, 'A Brief History of the Blood: The Story of the Blood of Christ in Transatlantic Evangelical Devotion,' *Evangelical Review of Theology* 31/3 (2007): 242.
23. Zinzendorf, 'Litany of the Wounds of the Husband', quoted in Craig D. Atwood, *Community of the Cross: Moravian Piety in Colonial Bethlehem* (University Park: Pennsylvania State University Press, 2004), 1.

Not surprisingly, the explicit, evocative and erotic quality of this devotional culture created controversy, in spite of Zinzendorf's rather disingenuous defence of it as orthodox Lutheran practice.

Use of the Litany was short-lived, and after Zinzendorf's death the Moravian movement moved away from some of the more unusual aspects of his theology. Nonetheless, a belief in, and devotion to, the suffering and death of Christ as the only basis for salvation remained central to Moravian conviction and culture. A major collection of Moravian hymns, published in 1863 for use by Moravian brethren throughout the world, contained many hymns that focused on the suffering Christ, including his wounds.[24]

These hymns also modeled the emotions that could be expected throughout the Christian life. Hymns on 'Self-Knowledge and Sighing for Grace' included verses like the following:

> Lord, thy body's Saviour,
> Comfort us anew;
> Ah, regard our weeping;
> Thy compassion show:
> Pardon our transgressions,
> Hear our fervent cry,
> And our souls and bodies
> Heal and sanctify.[25]

In a section on 'Patience and Confidence in God,' the hymns spoke of the joy that came with the assurance of sins forgiven, with lines such as 'How happy we, when guilt is gone;/ This alters our whole frame.'[26] Hymns were provided for those at every stage and in every state of life, including those facing death. A hymn in a section on 'Departure and Resurrection' began:

> Why do we mourn departing friends,
> Or shake at death's alarms?

---

24. See, for example, Hymn 316 and Hymn 804, *Liturgy and Hymns for the use of the Protestant Church of the United Brethren* (London: William Mallalieu & Co, 1863), np.
25. Hymn 524. *Liturgy and Hymns*, np.
26. Hymn 629. *Liturgy and Hymns*, np.

'Tis but the voice that Jesus sends
To call them to his arms.

This hymnbook demonstrated the ongoing Moravian culture of 'heart-religion'.

Recognising this theological and devotional context is illuminating for understanding many aspects of Moravian missionary practice. In the case of Moravian missionaries in Australia, one example will suffice to show the broader value of understanding this context. In his brilliant study of the conversion of Nathanael Pepper, an Aboriginal man who came into contact with Moravian missionaries at Ebenezer and then Ramahyuck, Robert Kenny has argued that the missionaries' emphasis on the suffering Jesus provided a significant point of cultural connection between Pepper and the missionaries. Specifically, Kenny notes that Pepper displayed a strong interest in the sufferings of Christ and that this was central to an experience in 1860 that the missionaries identified as his conversion. After hearing a sermon on Christ's agony in the garden of Gethsemane, Pepper came to the missionary Spieseke in distress, saying 'I have thought and thought how He went that night into the garden, and prayed there, till the sweat came down like drops of blood—and that for me'.[27]

Kenny suggests that the concept of Christ's saving blood may have been meaningful to Pepper because many Aboriginal spiritual traditions recognised blood as sacred and powerful. Kenny notes that blood is generally significant within Christian tradition, identifying it as the 'the sacred centre of Christian faith'.[28] He does not mention however, that blood was prominent in Moravian discourse and theology to an unusual extent. Where missionaries from other traditions might have focused on God as Creator in their initial preaching, Moravian tradition brought the sacrifice of Christ, and the physical expression of that sacrifice, front and centre. Pepper's conversion experience suggests that in his case at least, this proved a meaningful bridge between his own worldview and that of the German Moravian missionaries.

---

27. Quoted in Kenny, *The Lamb Enters the Dreaming*, 212.
28. Kenny, *The Lamb Enters the Dreaming*, 196.

Tears

Nathanael Pepper's response to the story of Christ's agony at Gethsemane was to weep. The missionary Spieseke interpreted these tears as signs of remorse.[29] Together, Pepper's words and display of emotion seemed to match perfectly with the Moravian ideal: pity at the suffering of Jesus produced guilt over one's sinfulness and eventually the assurance of sins forgiven. Undoubtedly, this was one of the main reasons why the missionaries found Pepper's profession of faith both convincing and encouraging.[30]

The Moravian response to Pepper's tears has broader implications. I have noted that in the European context, what Benjamin Pugh calls the 'essentially subjective nature of Moravian spirituality' meant that emotion was seen as a significant indicator of spiritual progress.[31] In cross-cultural contexts, where missionaries might often find the inner lives of Indigenous people profoundly inaccessible because of linguistic and cultural difference, emotions displayed in and through the body might provide particularly valuable external indicators of internal change.

This perspective explains why the Moravian missionaries who worked in Australia often noted in their writings examples of bodily displays of emotion by Aboriginal people. Emotional tones of voice, cries or tears were encouraging evidence of repentance. 'Today we had a proof that our labour is not in vain in the Lord' Spieseke wrote triumphantly. 'A candidate for baptism, named Brown, who had hitherto seemed too dull to comprehend the simplest things came to us, saying with emotion that "he loved the Lord who had died to save him," and requesting soon to be baptised.'[32] Of another man, Hagenauer wrote, 'About his own spiritual state he expressed himself very clearly and decidedly, saying that he grieved over his many and great sins, but rejoiced that he had found full pardon for all in the precious blood of Jesus.'[33] Spieseke wrote of Nathanael Pepper's brother, Philip, that 'he was awakened, and began to long for mercy, crying: "I am a poor sinner, but the Lord will accept me".'[34] Writing of a group of

---

29. Robert Kenny suggests that Pepper was more likely weeping for joy. *The Lamb Enters the Dreaming*, 212.
30. Kenny, *The Lamb Enters the Dreaming*, 214.
31. Pugh, 'A Brief History of the Blood', *op cit*, 242.
32. AW Spieseke, Report on Ebenezer, *Periodical Accounts*, (1866), 247.
33. F Hagenauer, Report on Ramahyuck, *Periodical Accounts*, (1877), 211.
34. AW Spieseke, Report on Ebenezer, *Periodical Accounts*, (1874).

boys who had come to repent of bad behaviour, Matilda Ward, the Moravian matron at Mapoon noted 'All in tears'.[35]

Missionaries also sought evidence of joy that demonstrated gratitude for the sacrifice of Jesus and the assurance of sins forgiven. Ward wrote delightedly of one young woman, Annette, who 'came with beaming face' to say 'Auntie, I decided this afternoon to be on Christ's side & I feel so happy and I have come to tell you'.[36] On rare occasions, missionaries were able to record times when large numbers of Aboriginal mission residents displayed such emotional responses, as when Ward wrote of Mapoon in 1912:

> Boys & girls, Men & women under the Power of the Holy Spirit. Many have taken their stand on Christ's side ... Some come with joy depicted on their faces—others in sorrow for past sins & others again desirous to know more of Jesus & His love.[37]

When telling a young man named Jack that he could be baptised, Hagenauer noted 'it was delightful to see how his face brightened up'.[38]

As these examples show, missionaries scrutinised Aboriginal people closely, paying attention to their bodily appearance as well as their words, for emotional clues as to their spiritual state. This applied not only to the process of conversion, but to the whole of life and also to death. Deathbeds were particularly important, with the missionaries regularly noting cases of Aboriginal Christians who had displayed patience and calm assurance in the face of great suffering.[39] Such assurance provided welcome evidence of a saving faith. Of one death, Spieseke commented, 'To witness

---

35. March 11, 1912. Matilda Ward's diary. MSS 1893/11. BOEMAR Records, Mitchell Library.
36. Jan 28, 1912. Matilda Ward's diary. MSS 1893/11. BOEMAR Records, Mitchell Library.
37. 12-31 March, 1912. Matilda Ward's diary. MSS 1893/11. BOEMAR Records, Mitchell Library, Sydney.
38. F Hagenauer, Report on Ramahyuck, *Periodical Accounts* (1866), 198.
39. See, for example, Spieseke, Report on Ebenezer, *Periodical Accounts* (1866), 31. J Kuehn, Report on McLaren Vale, *Periodical Accounts* (1865), 38.

such a triumphantly-happy death is well calculated to revive our often feeble faith.'[40]

After the death of a mission resident had occurred, the emotional responses of the bereaved family and friends were also the focus of missionary scrutiny. For the Moravians, the strong expressions of grief that were part of Aboriginal funeral rituals were evidence of their 'heathen' state. Hagenauer listed the 'dismal howling around the graves of the dead' as a key element of the 'depraved' state of Aboriginal people prior to the arrival of missionaries.[41] Describing the funeral of a young girl at Ramahyuck as 'a very solemn occasion', Kramer noted:

> What a change from the former days, when in cases of death we had to tear from the women's hands the axes, spears, and knives with which they were cutting themselves, to show their sorrow and despair. In many gardens of the natives there are graves of little children, at which the poor mother may be seen quietly weeping for her departed treasure.[42]

Again, the bodily deportment of Aboriginal women was seen as evidence of spiritual progress, the change from 'despair' to quiet weeping indicated that these women did not 'mourn as those without hope'.

This quote from Kramer indicates that missionaries might, under certain circumstances, feel justified in interfering in Aboriginal expressions of emotion, as when they considered it appropriate to disrupt funeral ceremonies to 'tear from the women's hands' the implements with which they were expressing their grief. To be spiritually significant, however, the emotional responses that the missionaries looked for must be the result of inner, God-given transformation, not external pressure. Of course, missionaries sought to encourage such responses, through preaching, liturgy, rebuke and example. That such responses were rewarded by missionary approval was no doubt also significant in socialising mission residents into such behaviour, particularly for those people brought up on the missions from childhood. Nonetheless, missionaries themselves saw them-

---

40. Spieseke, Report on Ebenezer, *Periodical Accounts* (1868), 421.
41. Hagenauer, Report on Ramahyuck, *Periodical Accounts* (1876), 512.
42. Kramer, Report on Ramahyuck, *Periodical Accounts* (1872), 369.

selves as largely powerless to produce spiritually significant emotions in those they evangelised.

One clear indication of this is that missionaries repeatedly lamented that the emotions they considered appropriate were often not forthcoming. This particularly applied to displays of emotional distress that missionaries saw as the natural sign of repentance. Describing the death of one older woman in 1868, Spieseke commented that 'She had the "poor sinner's" feeling; the humble conviction of her guilt and unworthiness which is unhappily not commonly to be met with among these people.'[43] This was clearly disturbing to the missionaries, and in one report Spieseke reflected:

> In taking a review of the past year, I cannot complain as far as the blacks are concerned, their conduct having on the whole been good. Sometimes I feel, however, as if I had wrought in vain. I should like to see more spiritual life, more of the awakened earnestness, which urges a man to ask, 'What must I do to be saved?'[44]

Hagenauer commented similarly, that although the people at Ramahyuck were regular attenders at church, 'we would fain see more thirst after the waters of salvation and for this we pray continually'.[45] These comments demonstrate again that for the missionaries, 'spiritual life' was evidenced in part by particular emotional states, an 'awakened earnestness', not simply good conduct or church attendance. Where these states could not be detected, missionaries feared the lack of spiritual life.

Broadly speaking, the Moravian experience was not unusual. As Bruce Hindmarsh has noted, the spiritual experiences that European evangelicals of the eighteenth and nineteenth centuries saw as normative were in fact the product of European history and culture.[46] In different cultural contexts, people responded differently to the message that missionaries brought. This could be a disorienting and disturbing experience for missionaries.

---

43. Spieseke, Report on Ebenezer, *Periodical Accounts* (1868), 421.
44. Spieseke, Report on Ebenezer, *Periodical Accounts* (1875), 354.
45. Hagenauer, Report on Ramahyuck, *Periodical Accounts* (1866), 197.
46. Hindmarsh, *The Evangelical Conversion Narrative*, 329–342.

The Moravian missionaries in Australia responded to the lack of spiritually appropriate emotions that they perceived in Aboriginal people in a number of ways. At times, they simply hoped for the best, taking verbal avowals at face value. Kramer wrote of one young girl:

> On her deathbed she expressed a wish to go to our Saviour, in reply to our question, and we would indulge the hope that, although we could detect little evidence of sorrow for sin, the Saviour has graciously cleansed her from all sin and taken her to Himself.[47]

Several years later, in 1876, he commented with regards to five young Aboriginal men who had professed faith:

> We have reason to believe that their hearts have been touched, as well as their minds taught, and although there is not the striking conversion that is often witnessed in such as have grown up in heathenism, there is unquestionably the beginning of a work of grace in their hearts, which will, we trust, in increasing measure be manifested in devoted Christian lives.[48]

This cautious description of 'the beginning of a work of grace' in the hearts of young men is a far cry from the 'striking conversion' of Nathanael Pepper and others sixteen years earlier. It exemplifies, however, how Moravian missionaries sought to adapt their expectations to the realities they encountered in Australia, focusing on the verbal testimony or the evidence of 'devoted Christian lives' rather than emotion.

Race

Reflecting on Moravian missionaries' attitudes to bodily displays of emotion helps identify some of the ways in which a theological understanding can provide nuance to postcolonial readings of missionary behaviour. For example, Richard Eves, who I quoted at the outset of this article, does

---

47. Kramer, Report on Ramahyuck, *Periodical Accounts* (1872), 369.
48. Kramer, Report on Ebenezer, *Periodical Accounts* (1876), 512.

not distinguish between the 'civilised' and the 'Christianised' body, when he argues that missionaries sought to 'discipline' Indigenous bodies into an ideal of European respectability. Moravian missionaries explicitly affirmed the value of certain aspects of 'civilisation' and sought to inculcate these aspects among Aboriginal people on missions. In the case of emotion, however, they focused on a set of physical behaviours—weeping at the thought of a crucified Jesus, crying out at one's sinfulness, beaming with joy or dying in rapture—that had little to do with middle-class respectability. This is not to suggest that missionary understandings of emotion were not culturally constructed, but it is to argue that theology should be taken seriously, alongside factors like class and imperialist ideology, in understanding missionary behaviour and its impact on Indigenous individuals and cultures.

Recognising the significance of the theological assumptions that influenced Moravian behaviour also allows a more accurate recognition of of other influences on missionary understanding. The vast majority of missionary references to bodily displays of emotion among Aboriginal people in the texts I have studied are concerned with spiritual progress or decline. Emotional display, in these references, is not linked in any explicit way to race. There is also, however, some evidence of other ways of understanding emotion. Among Europeans who denied the fundamental unity of mankind, influenced by pre-Darwinist polygenist theories or, later, by social Darwinist notions of a hierarchy of races, it was common to argue that Aboriginal people were inherently incapable of civilisation or Christianisation.[49] Hagenauer, who became the most influential of the Moravian missionaries in Australia, occasionally referred to this debate in his reports and the terms in which he did so are significant. Specifically, he noted that the behaviour of Aboriginal Christians was proof against those who believed that Aboriginal people had 'no feelings of humanity or religion' or 'were devoid of any of the higher feelings of humanity'.[50] It seems entirely consistent with Moravian theology that Hagenauer would understand human unity in terms of a shared capacity to feel.

---

49. For a summary of the debate over these ideas in colonial Australia, and the significance of Pepper's conversion in this context, see Kenny, *The Lamb Enters the Dreaming*, 29–62.
50. Hagenauer, Reports on Ramahyuck, *Periodical Accounts* (1876), 60 and *Periodical Accounts* (1878), 381.

In Hagenauer's reports, the relationship between emotion and human nature was employed to defend Aboriginal capacity. However, the connection between particular feelings and human capacity could lead missionaries to offensive conclusions. Matilda Ward, in a private letter written to a Moravian bishop in 1906, commented on the recent departure of the mission assistant, a Pacific Islander named Peter Bee.

> He left us two days ago & we were all sorry to say Good-bye to him, his wife and child. They were in tears themselves. We find the Pacific Islanders much more affectionate than these Australian aboriginals are. I think without doubt we can say our people are the lowest of all.[51]

Such derogatory stereotyping directly paralleled the racial hierarchies being promulgated by the social Darwinism of this period, in which Pacific Islanders were considered marginally superior to Aboriginal people.[52] Though this type of comment was fairly rare in the writings of Moravian missionaries, it demonstrates how, in the colonial context, Moravian assumptions about emotion could be integrated with deeply oppressive racial ideologies.

Conclusion

Moravian missionaries who came to Australia brought with them a wide range of assumptions about human nature and progress. In this article I have made the simple though often ignored point that many of these assumptions were theological. In particular, Moravian theology led missionaries to assume that certain emotional states, identifiable through particular bodily displays, were a significant sign of spiritual progress. 'Heart-religion' was also a matter of the body.

---

51. Matilda Ward to Bishop LaTrobe, 20 April 1906. MF 187. Moravian Mission Papers, Australian Institute of Aboriginal and Torres Strait Islander Studies Library, Canberra.
52. For anthropological and missionary discussions of the racial characteristics of Pacific Islanders and Aboriginal people, see Helen Bethea Gardner, *Gathering for God: George Brown in Oceania* (Dunedin: Otago University Press, 2006), 114–120.

In retrospect, this universalising of emotion had very ambivalent implications. On the one hand, Moravian missionaries were robust defenders of Aboriginal humanity and spiritual capacity in the midst of a settler society that denied both. Bodily displays of emotion could provide a point of connection between missionaries and Indigenous people, which seemed to cut across language and cultural difference. On the other hand, Moravian understandings of emotion meant that Aboriginal people's bodies were scrutinised and evaluated on the basis of a very narrow, culturally specific understanding of appropriate emotion that was often unaware of or derogatory towards emotional norms within Indigenous culture. Undoubtedly, Aboriginal people responded with emotion to their encounters with missionaries, at times welcoming and at other times rejecting the words and actions of missionaries. Missionaries showed little awareness, however, that emotion and its bodily manifestations could be culturally constructed. Unless Aboriginal people displayed the physical signs that missionaries expected, their claims to faith could be questioned. At worst, missionaries could interpret Aboriginal responses within the racist hierarchies of the time. In the colonial context, this particular theology of the body could sometimes unify and sometimes divide.

Image-bearing cyborgs?

Stephen Garner

Stephen Garner
School of Theology, University of Auckland, New Zealand

Introduction

In recent times the figure of the cyborg has imposed itself upon Western technoculture through popular culture, and in sociological reflection within academia. The term 'cyborg' or 'cybernetic organism', coined by Manfred Clynes and Nathan Kline in the 1960s, was part of a proposal to technologically augment human beings (in particular, astronauts) to survive in harsh environments.[1] Drawing from this idea popular culture has often portrayed the cyborg figure as the literal fusion of the biological human being with inorganic technology, often to the detriment of human identity and dignity. Alternatively, in the academic world the cyborg represents a metaphor for exploring contemporary technoculture, existing as a hybrid figure that forms a nexus where existing categories used to organise the world collapse and restructure themselves. In both cases the cyborg inhabits in a new, constructed world that exists in the borderlands of more familiar cultural and experiential terrain.

The cyborg is a generator of 'narratives of apprehension' about technology and human technological proclivity. It stands in contrast to many of the traditional ways in which the world is ordered, and is a discon-

---

1. Manfred E Clynes and Nathan S Kline, 'Cyborgs and Space', in The Cyborg Handbook, edited by Chris Hables Gray (New York: Routledge, 1995), 29–33.

certing form that raises questions about human nature, human identity, the relationship between the human and non-human in the world, and in particularly how to live wisely and wholesomely in a world constantly being reshaped by technology. In the past few years religious and theological engagement with the concept of the cyborg has begun to emerge, particularly within discussions about bioethics.[2] This discussion has often been carried out in strident terms, tied into extreme visions of techno-pessimism and anxiety, and in doing so has failed to engage with the concept of human beings and the Christian tradition as being rich with images of hybridity that may provide helpful insight into engaging with the cyborg and technoculture constructively.[3]

In the following paper, the theological motif of human beings being made in the image and likeness of God found in the Judeo-Christian tradition will be used to engage with the figure of the cyborg. It is asserted that the *imago Dei* is realised in hybridity, and, in conjunction with other theological motifs, provides resources for living wisely in contemporary technoculture.

Cyborgs: Biological and Cultural

Discussions about the nature of the cyborg tend to take one of two approaches. The first of these might be thought of as the *biological* cyborg, where technologies interact with the physical nature of a human being with implications for human morphology, while the second, the *cultural* cyborg, functions as a metaphor through which human identity is determined through interaction with technoculture.

The biological cyborg describes an organism, typically human, who has had technological artifacts added to their physical being. Some technological implants are now taken almost for granted. Synthetic hip re-

---

2. Philip Hefner, *Technology and Human Becoming* (Minneapolis: Fortress Press, 2003); Anne Kull, 'Cyborg Embodiment and the Incarnation', *Currents in Theology and Mission* 28/3-4 (2001): 279-284; Anne Kull, 'Speaking Cyborg: Technoculture and Technonature', *Zygon* 37/2 (2002): 279-287.
3. Tal Brooke (ed), *Virtual Gods: The Seduction of Power and Pleasure in Cyberspace* (Eugene: Harvest House, 1997); Nigel M de S Cameron, 'The Pursuit of Enhancement: The Latest from Brave New Britain', *Christianity Today* http://www.christianitytoday.com/ct/2006/108/32.0.html (accessed 10 March 2006); C Christopher Hook, 'The Techno Sapiens Are Coming', *Christianity Today* 48/1 (2004): 36-40.

placements, pacemakers, heart valves and metal pins and plates for bone injuries have all become relatively common, as have a variety of reproductive technologies. Prosthetic work too is becoming more advanced with 'bionic' limbs becoming more of a reality.[4] While biotechnologies, such as genetic therapies, cloning, transgenics, xenotransplantation, and pharmaceutical products, are also becoming possibilities particularly in the area of medicine, along with digital neurological implants.

However, this biological interpretation of the cyborg has less impact than understanding it as a cultural or functional interpretation. For example, cognitive scientist Andy Clark asserts that human beings are 'natural-born cyborgs', in that they have an inherent inclination to form relationships with technologies that expand the human mind outside of the physical limitations of the physical body. In effect, the mind 'leaks' out into the technological tools and prostheses that human beings use in everyday life.

> For we shall be cyborgs not in the merely superficial sense of combining flesh and wires but in the more profound sense of being human-technology symbionts: thinking and reasoning systems whose minds and selves are spread across biological brain and nonbiological circuitry.[5]

Clark argues that it is a mistake to envisage that the most profound and intimate mergers of technology and the human being involve bodily penetration and, at times, replacement. Prostheses, neural implants, and enhanced perceptual and intellectual systems are the norm for the science fiction cyborg, but the impact of everyday appliances and devices such

---

4. Peter Menzel and Faith D'Aluisio, *Robo Sapiens: Evolution of a New Species* (Cambridge, MA: MIT Press, 2000), 178–181.
5. Andy Clark, *Natural-Born Cyborgs: Minds, Technologies, and the Future of Human Intelligence* (New York: Oxford University Press, 2003), 3. This way of viewing a human being's interaction with technology is similar to that proposed by Gregory Stock, who argues that human beings are 'fyborgs' (functional cyborgs), where technology is fused functionally, rather than physically, with the human person. The latter does occur in some instances, such as dental fillings, pacemakers, and artificial heart valves, but the issue is whether a technology is considered functionally part of the person. See Gregory Stock, *Redesigning Humans: Choosing Our Children's Genes* (London: Profile, 2002), 24–27.

as cell phones and wristwatches, is a more significant shaper of human identity and behaviour.[6]

Both cases, biological and cultural, highlight that technology can no longer be thought of as simply tools to be applied, but rather it is the environment in which we live and breathe and have our being.

Narratives of apprehension

The cyborg is a product of a work where boundaries between traditional categories that are used to organise the world are being lost under the pressure of technoculture. In particular, the lines that once seemed clear between organic and inorganic, animal and plant, human and machine, and male and female are no longer fixed and have begun to shift and blur.

In this world, the human-machine boundary is pressured by neurotechnologies, such as cochlear implants, which merge digital technology with the human nervous system. Transgenic fruit, vegetables and animals contest perceived boundaries in nature that distinguish species and kinds. Additionally, psychopharmaceuticals that reshape aspects of personality start to become lifestyle choices rather than therapies, while xenotransplantation, merging non-human tissue with human, is proposed as a beneficial therapy but carries with it challenges to both individual and communal human identity.[7] The ongoing developments of social virtual environments such as *Second Life*, together with other forms of mediated communication and social networking, also blur boundaries by allowing

---

6. Clark, *Natural-Born Cyborgs*, 27–28.
7. For example, in 2005 *Toi te Taiao: the Bioethics Council* engaged in discussion about the spiritual, ethical and cultural aspects of xenotransplantation within the New Zealand context, including the possible implications for Maori identity sourced in *whakapapa* (genealogy) and *whanau* (family). For the discussion documents see *The Cultural, Spiritual and Ethical Aspects of Xenotransplantation: Animal-to-Human Transplantation: A Discussion Document*, (Wellington: Toi te Taiao: the Bioethics Council, 2005); *Whakapapa & Xenotransplantation: Animal-to-Human Transplantation*, (Wellington: Toi te Taiao: the Bioethics Council, 2005). See also the report summarising the dialogue: *The Cultural, Ethical and Spiritual Aspects of Animal-to-Human Transplantation: A Report on Xenotransplantation* (Wellington: Toi te Taiao: the Bioethics Council, 2005).

people to construct multiple identities that may reshape, or even eliminate, aspects such as gender, race and age.[8]

The pressure exerted by this blurring of traditional boundaries leads to what might be called 'narratives of apprehension' about human technological proclivity and its impact upon individual human beings, human communities, and the wider world. In particular, apprehension captures a mix of anxiety and wonder in the face of new technological developments. There is anxiety about the negative effects of a particular technology, in actuality or in potentiality, as well as anxieties that the benefits promised by technology, such as the eradication of a disease, might be thwarted.

Parallel to these anxious accounts are those that capture a sense of wonder and awe at the power and scope of human technological agency. This is the realisation of the potentially wonderful, helpful and world-changing possibilities through human agency in the world, which can fire the imagination of individuals and communities.

As well as this passive sense of anxiety and wonder found within individuals and communities there is also the sense of apprehension as being an activity, where technology is wrestled with, sometimes physically, but also in the struggle to understand concepts, ideas or emotions in the engagement with technology.

Nowhere are these accounts of apprehension played out more clearly though than within the speculative or science fiction, both in literary and cinematic formats, that find their roots in the Greek myths of Prometheus and Icarus, and in the medieval Jewish tale of the Golem of Prague.

Within literature we encounter Mary Shelly's *Frankenstein* (1818) produced in a time when human apprehension about the future, in both its negative and positive senses, was taking place in a new culture of scientific, rational and technological development, and questions are being raised about being created yet being creators, and the boundaries between organism and machine, human and non-human.[9]

---

8. Linden Research Inc, 'Second Life: Your World. Your Imagination.' http://secondlife.com/ (accessed 15 September 2006); Veronika Schlör, 'Cyborgs: Feminist Approaches to the Cyberworld', *Concilium* 1 (2005): 60–67; Sherry Turkle, *Life on the Screen: Identity in the Age of the Internet* (New York: Touchstone, 1997), 177–180.
9. Elaine Graham, *Representations of the Post/Human: Monsters, Aliens and Others in Popular Culture* (Manchester: Manchester University Press, 2002), 14.

This century dystopian critiques such as Aldous Huxley's *Brave New World* (1932) and George Orwell's *Nineteen Eighty-Four* (1949), which assert the potential for technology to reshape society negatively through the application of biotechnology and mass media respectively, are joined by more recent writers such as William Gibson, *Neuromancer* (1984), and Neal Stephenson, *Snow Crash* (1992). The latter authors defining the genre of 'cyberpunk', where information technology, virtual reality, mythology and consumerism meet also in a dystopian view of the near future characterised by technological impact as alarming, violent, and in many ways dehumanising. These apprehensive visions carry over into cinema, with a continuing series of films over the past fifty years portraying concern over the impact of atomic power, information technology, and biotechnology.[10]

These contemporary narratives highlight what Lelia Green calls 'the widespread fascination with the interface of biology and technology, and the potential for fusion between the two.' It is in these types of stories that society explores the boundaries of what it means to be human and tries to distil the essence of humanness. Questions about how to live and how to be human are addressed, as well as the hopes and fears of people who are increasingly dependent on technology and the cultures it creates. There is, she asserts, almost an enthrallment with the question of how much technology compromises the essentially human.[11] Does a pacemaker or a cochlear implant make one less human? Have the current abilities of reproductive science, organ transplants and cultured tissue already crossed forbidden boundaries? And, for those within religious communities, how do their theological or religious understandings of the ordering of the world respond to these boundary issues?

These narratives of apprehension are set within what might be seen as a much wider series of disruptive changes to humanity's self-perception of itself and its place in the world. The Copernican Revolution shifted the geocentric universe to a heliocentric one, challenging traditional medieval cosmology, while later Newtonian models portraying the universe appeared to following rules in a similar fashion to a machine. Not only

---

10. For example, *Them!* (1954); *Colossus: The Forbin Project* (1970); *The China Syndrome* (1979); *WarGames* (1983); *Jurassic Park* (1993); *Gattaca* (1997); *The Truman Show* (1998); *The Matrix* (1999); *AI Artificial Intelligence* (2000); and *I, Robot* (2004).
11. Lelia Green, *Technoculture: From Alphabet to Cybersex* (Crowsnest, NSW: Allen and Unwin, 2002), 167.

were human beings not the centre of the universe, they might be just cogs in a vast machine.

These cosmological challenges were followed by others offered by the natural sciences of the nineteenth century, particularly those raised by Charles Darwin in his *Origin of the Species* (1859). Evolutionary theory, popularised by Darwin's work, now linked humanity firmly into the biosphere, again challenging humanity's self-image. Further developments socially and culturally, such as economic ideologies that saw human beings in terms of economic units or populations of consumers, also contributed to how human beings thought about themselves. More recently, developments such as the discovery of the structure of DNA in the 1950s, and the consequent mapping of the human genome in the last few years, together with insights from the fields of cognitive sciences, neurology and computer science, create the climate for yet another shift in understanding who we are as human beings.

The overall trajectory of these events leads to an environment where technology, such as biotechnology, is viewed in a myriad of different ways within society. For example, Celia Deane-Drummond and others identify that there are some significant concerns being expressed by the general public about biotechnology, and about genetically modified organisms and food in particular. These concerns tend to differ from those envisaged by those charged with overseeing or implementing policy, or with researching and developing biotechnology. Rather they reflect questions that are concerned with the very essence of human personhood, about human nature, and the character of the relationship between human beings and the natural world. Commenting on public resistance and antipathy towards particular forms of biotechnology in Britain and Europe at the end of the 1990s they write,

> It seems conceivable that the intensity of current controversies around genetically modified crops and foods arises in part from the fact that, in their regulation in the public do-

main, *conflicting ontologies of the person* are making themselves felt in the politics of everyday life.[12]

Issues raised by the general public tend not to be focused upon a narrow evaluation of whether a particular technological development is safe or low-risk decided on a case-by-case basis, but are instead related to broader issues. Questions are often raised about the direction that this technology is leading in general, along with those about the motivations of those in power, who are implementing policy and technological development. Furthermore, in their studies of public opinion, issues surrounding what assumptions are being made about the relationship between humans and nature, and about human nature itself, were often significant, leading to tensions between views portrayed as wholly 'scientific' and others which included those views along with other 'lay' ones.

However, concerns about interfering in nature or challenging the notion of the human person were also held in tension with the idea that human beings have always used technology to shape the natural world and themselves. So biotechnological approaches that were perceived as therapeutic were better received than those that seemed to be implemented merely to increase productivity for the sake of profit. Ultimately, the questions raised concerned not only human ontology and the challenging of a perceived natural order, but also how to live wisely and well in a technological world.[13]

Thus, the figure of the cyborg and the hybrid is an ambivalent one in this world of shifting boundaries, where technological manipulation of the world relies upon there being some kind of consistent structure or order to affect, and yet in doing so existing notions of some kind of fixed ordering to the natural world are challenged or rejected. As Elaine Graham notes,

---

12. Celia Deane-Drummond, Robin Grove-White, and Bronislaw Szerszynski, 'Genetically Modified Theology: The Religious Dimensions of Public Concerns About Agricultural Biotechnology', *Studies in Christian Ethics* 14/2 (2001): 27. See also Jesper Lassen and Andrew Jamison, 'Genetic Technologies Meet the Public: The Discourses of Concern', *Science, Technology, & Human Values* 31/1 (2006): 8–28.
13. Deane-Drummond *et al*, 'Genetically Modified Theology', *op cit*, 25–31.

Yet to speak of an orderliness to nature, of its integrity as a mediation of divine purpose, is not the same as inferring an immutability to nature which forbids the 'unnatural' interventions of technology or cultural diversity. So we must be ware of attributing to 'nature' a fixity and purpose—or even a homogeneity and determinism—which it does not possess. Human relationships to nature are altogether more complex, and appeals to what is 'natural' provide little help when, as in the age of advanced biotechnology, this is the very category which is revealed to be malleable and problematic.[14]

Techno-optimistic social visions

Against this anxiety about human technological endeavour are the techno-optimistic visions of those who see great benefit and potential in the convergence of key technologies. This convergence brings with it stories and hopes wrapped up in a social vision of a world where human beings live out long lives enriched by technology that provides wholeness, health and personal fulfilment. Individuals and communities are transformed, and the human spirit and intellect, mediated by technology, bring about a new world that bears a startling resemblance to a vision of heaven on earth.

This vision of a new world forms a significant theme in the report *Converging Technologies for Improving Human Performance* produced by Mihail Roco and William Sims Bainbridge. Within the report, the authors paint an extremely optimistic picture of possible future human existence brought about through a technological renaissance delivered by the unfettered application of nanotechnology, biotechnology, information technology and cognitive science. These four key technologies will 'converge' to bring about a currently unheard of social, economic and military bounty for the United States, and by implication, the rest of the world.

> Moving forward simultaneously along many of these paths could achieve a golden age that would be a turning point for human productivity and quality of life. Technological conver-

---

14. Elaine Graham, 'Bioethics after Posthumanism: Natural Law, Communicative Action and the Problem of Self-Design', *Ecotheology* 9/2 (2004): 184–185.

gence could become the framework for human convergence. The twenty-first century could end in world peace, universal prosperity, and evolution to a higher level of compassion and accomplishment. It is hard to find the right metaphor to see a century into the future, but it may be that humanity would become like a single, distributed and interconnected 'brain' based in new core pathways of society. This will be an enhancement to the productivity and independence of individuals, giving them greater opportunities to achieve personal goals.[15]

This is the world desired by those who identify themselves as techno-progressive and transhumanist, the latter being an ideology that human beings can now use technology to control their own evolution and destiny, becoming, to all intents and purposes, god-like.

With roots in humanist and Enlightenment thinking, transhumanism is an emerging and broadly based philosophy, bioethic, cultural phenomenon whose proponents believe that technology can and should be applied to improve the human condition. Transhumanists believe that humanity ought to enter into a post-Darwinian phase of existence where intelligences, rather than the blind forces of natural selection, are in control of their own evolution.[16]

The transhumanist vision is an end-product of the belief that the human condition can be improved through reason, science and technology. It focuses predominantly upon the autonomous human individual, asserting the primacy of reason as a force for personal and therefore social transformation. Through the use of applied reason, values such as rational thinking, freedom, tolerance, and concern for others are increased. Ultimately,

---

15. Mihail C Roco and William Sims Bainbridge (eds), *Converging Technologies for Improved Human Performance: Nanotechnology, Biotechnology, Information Technology and Cognitive Science* (Arlington, VA: National Science Foundation/Department of Commerce, 2002), 6.
16. George Dvorsky, 'Better Living through Transhumanism', *The Humanist* 64/3 (2004): 7.

this leads to an ever-increasing improvement of the human condition. In this way, transhumanism offers the hope of a better world.[17]

These technologically based convictions parallel similar theological ones that assert that all is not right with the world, and that a better, more fully realised world or society is possible. In one sense, the social visions of the transhumanist function as a kind of technological eschatology, providing hope and meaning for those within the transhumanist community. Political theologian Duncan Forrester observes that this kind of utopianism generates goals and momentum toward the future and raises a 'horizon of meaning within which a society exists, policies are formulated, and actions taken.' This framework of meaning then provides the basis for moral and ethical consideration for those who are captured by this eschatological vision.[18]

The transhumanist social visions are one possible direction the energies of humans might take, and elements of it echo themes within Christian social visions. Certainly, the aim of alleviating suffering and sickness, and promoting personal fulfilment, can resonate with aspects of Christian themes of loving and serving others. However, what are the possible sources of interaction between these technological worlds of the cyborg and the Christian tradition?

Intersections with the Christian tradition

Some, such as sociologist Brenda Brasher, argue that institutional religions, such as Christianity, with their dependence upon pastoral and agrarian imagery and symbols found in their religious texts and imagination will struggle to address the world of the cyborg. At one level, religion must respond to the existential questions of the age, to boundary questions such as life and death, gender, bodily augmentation and transgenic modification that are created in light of new technologies. Additionally, religion must also address the issue of how human beings should live, through the

---

17. Nick Bostrom, 'The Transhumanist FAQ: A General Introduction', World Transhumanist Association http://www.transhumanism.org/resources/FAQv21.pdf (accessed 1 November 2004). (§1.1)
18. Duncan B Forrester, 'The Scope of Public Theology', *Studies in Christian Ethics* 17/2 (2004): 14. See also Douglas Meeks comments on ethical living as a consequence of eschatology in Jürgen Moltmann's theology of hope. M Douglas Meeks, *Origins of the Theology of Hope* (Philadelphia: Fortress Press, 1974), 47–49.

creation of symbols, stories and images that describe the world and life-giving behaviour within it.[19]

However, to reduce religious traditions, and Christianity in particular, to inflexible systems that do not have the resources to grapple with the figure of the cyborg, as Brasher does, is untrue. The cyborg, by definition, is a figure of hybridity, and the Christian tradition has within it a range of sources that deal with ambiguity and possibility within the notion of the hybrid. Examples within the Christian tradition include the understanding of God as triune; the paradox of the incarnation that unites Jesus Christ's human and divine natures in hypostatic union; eschatological frameworks that see the Kingdom of God as inaugurated, yet awaiting fullness; tensions between sin and grace in individuals and communities; and anthropologies that see human beings as occupying ambiguous or contested spaces between the categories of matter and spirit, as well as in bearing the *imago Dei*. The *imago Dei*, in particular, serves as a useful example when contemplating technological apprehension and hybridity.

The doctrine of *imago Dei*, that human beings somehow bear the image and likeness of God, has traditionally been one of the core aspects of various Christian anthropologies. Sourced primarily in the creation account in Genesis 1, the doctrine asserts that God intentionally creates humankind in God's own image and after God's own likeness (Gen 1:26-27) and then humanity is given a mandate to act within and upon the created order (Gen 1:28).

Within Christian theology these assertions have lead to three main views of the *imago Dei* being proposed. Firstly, that the image is substantive, reflecting God in the physical, psychological or metaphysical aspects of the human person. Secondly, that the image is relational, of importance in relationships vertically between God and the human person and horizontally between human beings. And thirdly, that the image is manifested functionally, in that human beings act as God or God's agents within creation because they bear God's image.

In recent years support for the third position, the image-as-function, has strengthened significantly, supported by the work of ancient Near Eastern researchers on the background of the motif, as well as by current

---

19. Brenda E Brasher, *Give Me That Online Religion* (New Brunswick, NJ: Rutgers University Press, 2004), 151–156.

Old Testament scholarship.[20] The human being is present upon the earth, firstly, to declare that the earth is the Lord's, secondly, to represent God within this world in a capacity of vice-regent or steward, and thirdly, to demonstrate that human agency is intimately tied to God's agency.

This form of the *imago Dei* lends itself to the concept of human beings as embodied creatures that are caught up in an intimate web of relationships within the natural world that birthed them. Thus, the *imago Dei* is connected to creatures exercising finite power and responsibility within a world with which they have solidarity.

To rely upon the functional model alone would be short-sighted. The declaration that human beings are made in the image and likeness of God, in order to represent and act for God within creation, is intimately tied to the concept of relationship. The *imago Dei* is not something that humankind innately grasps through its own devices and effects. Rather, the *imago Dei* is a designation that is sourced in the Triune God as the one who bestows that identity. Therefore, image bearing is intimately tied to representing the one who calls humankind into this role. Following Jürgen Moltmann, humanity can only represent and reflect God's glory in creation through an awareness of this relationship that calls forth a response.[21] This awareness might then be linked to a substantive dimension to the *imago Dei*, perhaps similar to Emil Brunner's formal image or Augustine's *capax Dei*, that works with the primary role of functionality situated in a relational context.

Furthermore, the *imago Dei* is linked intimately to the rest of the cosmos. Relationship with the divine is now also joined by a human relationship with wider creation. Human beings are creatures, even if they are called to be God's representatives in this world, and as such are dependent upon the world around them, a world that includes human and non-human, animate and inanimate, organism and machine. A finite image-bearing humanity is caught up with living and acting as God within this world, while simultaneously being dependent upon that world.

Perhaps then, the *imago Dei* should be understood in a manner similar to José Miguez Bonino's 'catholic' understanding that embraces elements

---

20. Gunnlaugur A Jónsson, *The Image of God: Genesis 1:26–28 in a Century of Old Testament Research* (Stockholm Sweden: Almqvist & Wiksell, 1988), 219–220.
21. Jürgen Moltmann, *God in Creation: An Ecological Doctrine of Creation*, trans. Margaret Kohl (London: SCM Press, 1985), 215–224.

of each of the three main interpretations to create a hybrid model of the *imago Dei*. Firstly, the *imago Dei* incorporates a dialectical aspect, which allows the human person to be a free and responsible being that can enter into genuine communion with God. To this is added a functional aspect, in that the human being is called to cultivate and care for the natural world, which is extended by a relational aspect that argues we become fully human through the expression of love to others. Together the combination of human-divine, human-human, and human-nature interactions make up the image."

Bonino's interpretation is centred on a dialectical aspect of human nature that primarily undergirds the call to creation care to be lived out in communities of love. However, if the functional dimension of the image is seen as having priority then that dimension, with its call to represent God and to reflect God's glory within creation, might serve as a better foundation, with the substantive and relational dimensions then nuancing its interpretation. For example, that while called to act as agents of God in the world, human beings should not do that in a way that is divorced from acting in loving and just ways, nor in ways that fail to recognise human existence as co-dependent with the wider natural world they are embodied within.

This interpretation of *imago Dei* correlates with the narratives of purpose and creativity expressed within technology. The narrative of purpose, of problem solving to improve the human condition, now becomes broadened to include human agency acting in such a way as to benefit both human beings and the wider creation that humanity is integrated within. This is tied to recognition that the natural world is of value to God and that human agency within this world should reflect that. Furthermore, it is a call to wise living but not necessarily the Baconian vision of a return to Eden, nor a utopian vision. Rather, it is the recognition that finite, created and limited humanity is called in some way to act as God's agents in the world, according to God's purposes for creation.

The narrative of creativity is also picked up in this vision of the *imago Dei*. Human beings image a God who creates and re-creates, and human beings play a role transforming creation, and even inject novelty into the

---

22. José Miguez Bonino, *Room to Be People: An Interpretation of the Message of the Bible for Today's World*, translated by Vickie Leach (Geneva: World Council of Churches, 1975), 31–33.

world, through exercising their capacities in areas such as art, science, and technology.

The correlation between the *imago Dei* and these technological narratives goes beyond a view that might be considered limited to an Old Testament interpretation of the *imago Dei*. The Christian tradition contains within it a teleological or eschatological trajectory that finds itself centred on Jesus Christ, the image of the invisible God, and into whose likeness the children of God are being transformed. This adds a redemptive perspective to the *imago Dei*, and indeed to the whole perception of God's activity within creation, that is extremely significant. This intersects with the previous correlation between the *imago Dei* and technological narratives of creativity and purpose, for now the narratives can be reframed within a redemptive context, where human beings image in their own way creative love that echoes that which God expresses to the world.

This redemptive theme does not argue that ultimate salvation can be achieved by technology but that redemptive activity linked to healing and wholeness, to 'shalom', can be tied to an *imago Dei* being developed and drawn toward the future by Christ. It is an engagement with a world that is caught in the eschatological tension that exists between the resurrection of Jesus Christ and the consummation of history at the eschaton.

This situation embraces technology and human agency within the love ethic of Jesus Christ: to love one another. The vision of the Kingdom of God, to love one another, is borne out incarnationally. Thus, the idea that human beings are made in this particular image of God can be seen in the human calling to embodied co-creation with God in a way that expresses this love ethic in a world that is caught in the eschatological 'already, but not yet' tension—itself a source of both wonder and apprehension.

This predominantly functional way of understanding the *imago Dei* has been appropriated within contexts engaging with technology through the theological metaphor of human beings as 'created co-creators'. Initially developed by Lutheran theologian Philip Hefner, the metaphor of the created co-creator has become embedded in a significant part of the theological engagement concerning relationships between human beings and technology.[23]

The 'created' aspect of the metaphor asserts the creaturehood of the human being as caused, created, dependent, finite, and not self-generating. There is a qualitative difference between Creator and creature, though the intentional creation of the world speaks of intimate relationship between the two. Therefore, humans should not consider themselves as conquerors of the cosmos, but instead as creatures that serve the creator, and as such find their identity sourced in their Creator.

The second aspect, 'co-creator', speaks though of a calling to act as an agent within the natural world. The 'co-' aspect reflects that, while the human is never the equal of God, God has produced humanity in such a way as to be part of the purposeful creative process in the cosmos. The human being is an agent working with, and for God. Hefner summarises his proposal as follows:

> Human beings are God's created co-creators whose purpose is to be the agency, acting in freedom, to birth the future that is most wholesome for the nature that has birthed us—the nature that is not only our own genetic heritage, but also the entire human community and the evolutionary and ecological reality in which and to which we belong. Exercising this agency is said to be God's will for humans.[24]

Typically, the metaphor occurs in discussions relating to biotechnology and medicine,[25] but it is also seen in reflections upon artificial

---

23. Philip Hefner, *The Human Factor: Evolution, Culture and Religion*, Theology and the Sciences (Minneapolis: Fortress Press, 1993).
24. Philip Hefner, *The Human Factor*, 27.
25. Ronald Cole-Turner, 'Is Genetic Engineering Co-Creation?', *Theology Today* 44/3 (1987): 338–349; Ulf Görman, 'Co-Creation or Hubris? Response to Biotechnology in Christianity, Judaism and Islam', in *Creative Creatures: Values and Ethical Issues in Theology, Science and Technology*, edited by Ulf Görman, Willem B Drees, and Hubert Meisinger (London: T&T Clark, 2005), 134–151; Bart Hansen and Paul Schotsmans, 'Cloning: The Human as Created Co-Creator?', *Ethical Perspectives* 8/2 (2001): 75–89; Ted Peters, 'Genes, Creation, and Co-Creation', *CTNS Bulletin* 13/1 (1993): 23–27.

intelligence,[26] ecology and social justice,[27] the motif of the cyborg,[28] ecclesiology,[29] incarnation,[30] and evolutionary theory.[31] The metaphor's inherent optimism about human creativity, and technology in particular, often lead to it being used to draw conclusions to support the particular technological activity in question, albeit with some caveats. Most often the motif is used in passing, either as a brief explanation of why human beings create technology, or as a potential base for the construction of ethical system for engagement with technology.[32]

The metaphor is not without its detractors, particularly those critics who see it as elevating the 'co-creation' aspect of the human being above that of the created, as 'baptising' all technological endeavour, as well as those who would question elements of the biocultural evolutionary scheme Hefner later imposed upon the theological scheme.[33] These critics highlight that technology in all its aspects must be truly engaged with, not just used or interacted with, through this metaphor. However, the metaphor does serve as a useful starting point, both as an example of a theological hybridity in its combination of finitude and freedom, and

---

26. Anne Foerst, *God in the Machine: What Robots Teach Us About Humanity and God* (New York: Dutton, 2004), 35–38; Noreen Herzfeld, 'Co-*Creator* or *Co*-Creator? The Problem with Artificial Intelligence', in *Creative Creatures: Values and Ethical Issues in Theology, Science and Technology*, edited by Ulf Görman, Willem B Drees, and Hubert Meisinger, Issues in Science and Theology (London: T&T Clark, 2005), 45–52.
27. Ann Pederson, 'The Not-Too-Distant Future: The Created Co-Creator', *Currents in Theology and Mission*, 28/3-4 (2001): 267–272.
28. Kull, 'Cyborg Embodiment', *op cit*, 279–287; Kull, 'Speaking Cyborg: Technoculture and Technonature', *op cit*, 279–287; Taede Smedes, 'Technology and Evolution: The Quest for a New Perspective', *Dialog* 44/4 (2005): 354–364.
29. Roger A Willer, 'Created Co-Creator in the Perspective of Church and Ethics', *Zygon* 39/4 (2004): 841–858.
30. Manuel G Doncel, 'The Kenosis of the Creator and of the Created Co-Creator', *Zygon* 39/4 (2004): 791–800.
31. Williams Irons, 'An Evolutionary Critique of the Created Co-Creator Concept', *Zygon* 39/4 (2004): 773–790.
32. For example, Graham, 'Bioethics after Posthumanism', *op cit*, 194–195.
33. Ronald Cole-Turner, *The New Genesis: Theology and the Genetic Revolution* (Louisville: Westminster/John Knox Press, 1993), 101–102. Other critics who see the 'co-creator' aspect as raising humanity to a inappropriate level with God include Peter Scott, 'The Technological Factor: Redemption, Nature, and the Image of God', *Zygon* 35/2 (2000): 371-383; Ng Kam Weng, 'Co-Creator or Priestly Steward: Theological Perspectives on Biotechnology', in *Beyond Determinism and Reductionism: Genetic Science and the Person*, edited by Mark LY Chan and Roland Chia (Adelaide: ATF Press, 2003), 75–94.

highlighting the two key aspects present in functional interpretations of the *imago Dei* that intersect with technological activity.

Conclusions—the image-bearing cyborg

Where, then, should hope be found in the face of technological apprehension? If to be human is to bear God's image and likeness, then hope is to be found in that calling. The *imago Dei*, seen through metaphors such as the created co creator, contains within it an explanation of human beings as inherently technological, and a trajectory that human technological agency should take. As such, it provides answers to the existential questions that arise out of apprehension's wonder and anxiety, and also provides wisdom for living within technoculture. Moreover, these answers can be framed using the language of the cyborg and the hybrid present within technocultural discourse.

A balanced emphasis upon dimensions of the created co-creator metaphor leads to an engagement with technology that seeks appropriate solutions to problems through novelty and creativity. The appropriateness takes into account not just the technological problem to be solved, but also the environment it takes place within, the individuals and communities that will be affected, the values that are present within the discourse around the technology, and whether it reflects God through the actions of the image-bearers involved. Thus, creativity is mediated through an understanding God who embodies love and compassion, a valuing of what is being created and of the physical world, and is responsive to others. An unbalanced focus upon either one of the aspects of the created co-creator can lead towards overly optimistic and pessimistic views of technology.

Emphasis upon the 'co-creator' aspect of image bearing favours an optimistic view of technology. Because human beings are called to a vocation of agency in the natural world, that agency is inherently good, and all technological activity will be ultimately working towards greater good in the world. This type of emphasis is evident within transhumanism. Even if it is not expressed explicitly within a Christian theology, their optimistic views of human technological ability's to reshape the world into a better place form religious narratives and social visions of hope and meaning. Questions of social concern and justice, the nature and potential of technologically generated risks, and the power of these narratives of self-improvement must be taken into account.[34]

Positively, the focus upon co-creation emphasises the narratives of purpose and creativity found within the Christian tradition. There is a call to act in purposeful and creative ways within the natural world in ways that are wholesome to others, acting with beneficence whenever possible. This highlights the aspects of awe and wonder located within apprehension over technology, recognising that 'technology, for all its good, is constantly on the edge of sin, exploitation, and greed. It is, after all, *human technology,* beset by our weaknesses.'[35] Human beings are capable of exerting tremendous ingenuity and power within the world, an observation that intersects with the understanding of the *imago Dei* declaring God's intention for humanity to be creative agents in the world, and also with the ways in which humanity can pursue that agency for its own agendas.

However, emphasis upon human agency that fails to recognise the finitude present within the 'created' aspect of human nature can lead toward narratives of oppression and anxiety. Technological eschatologies with their desire for transcendence over the material world assert that human salvation and destiny is within humanity's hands alone. This rejection of human finitude is often coupled with a deeply held individualism that fails to recognise the embodied human being as embedded within a web of interdependencies in the wider world. Relationships with human beings and other parts of the natural world can become reduced to what those entities contribute in terms of utility, if they are considered at all, losing any sense that they might have intrinsic moral value or rights outside of that utility.

Theologically, the themes of social justice, embodiment and redemption being ultimately within God's hands resist this overt technological optimism. Transhumanism's quest for longevity, cyborgs, artificial intelligence and virtual reality may ultimately be within the divine plan, however the criteria by which it should be evaluated goes beyond personal choices and cost/benefit analyses.

---

34. Stephen R Garner, 'Transhumanism and Christian Social Concern', *Journal of Evolution and Technology* 14/2 (2005).
35. Cole-Turner, The New Genesis, 102.

For those who downplay co-creation, and instead emphasise the 'createdness' aspect of human being, there is the danger that technology becomes perceived too negatively. This rejects the calling present within the *imago Dei* to be human through creative, technological agency. The desire to avoid 'playing God' can lead to the situation of not 'playing human', and a denial of technology as a viable avenue for God to work through to bring about a measure of wholeness in the world.

Pessimistic views of technology rightly highlight the negative potential that generates much of the 'anxiety' present within apprehension. This anxiety it to be welcomed, for it demonstrates the very real possibility that technologies, and technoculture with all its various dimensions, can be unjust and damaging to relationships between individuals, communities and their environments. As such, this anxiety calls for the recognition and voices of those unjustly affected, and for others to speak on their behalf if they have no voice. Theologically, the pessimistic voices also underline humanity's inability to bring true wholeness into the world through its own efforts, and the potential for evil as well as for good in all aspects of human agency.

If the pessimists critique technology by emphasising human finitude and limitedness, and the optimists stress the potential in technology for good and human transcendence, then hope is to be found in a hybrid position that embraces both dimensions. Interpreting the image bearing human being as the created co-creator, shaped by the imperatives to do justice, love kindness and walk humbly with God, allows both apprehension's awe and anxiety to be redirected into a hopeful narrative. Theologically, human beings can understand themselves as creators of technology and technoculture because they bear the *imago Dei*. The drive to act purposefully and creatively in the world is borne out of a vocation given by God to represent God in the world, and act within that world on God's behalf.

Furthermore, the *imago Dei* offers insight into how this agency is to be worked out in practice. The calling to represent God through activity reflects God's concern for the world and those within it. The *imago Dei* speaks of a humanity that has been intentionally created as an embodied part of a natural world that is of value to God, and which is part of God's redemptive plans. This embodiment is seen in humanity's biological dimension that speaks of a solidarity and interconnectedness with the rest of the natural world. Thus, agency is carried out in a medium that highlights human finitude and dependence, a point that is reiterated by the underlying materialism present in much of transhumanism.

The presence of narratives of hope does not (and should not) eliminate the narratives of apprehension present within contemporary technoculture. Hope arises from the theological reflection of the tension between wonder and anxiety, as each informs the other, and drives to the fore essential questions about human technological agency. It is essential to have avenues for raising, discussing and answering these questions in order to provide hope in the face of this tension between awe and anxiety. Narratives of hope do not displace those of apprehension but rather exist in symbiosis, allowing apprehension to serve a positive purpose in society. Thus, the narrative of apprehension generated by public unease about something like genetically-modified foodstuffs need not lead to futile acceptance of the situation, but instead energise those affected to examine why both wonder and anxiety are raised, and to act in ways that seek to bring about wholeness in that situation.

When these things are considered, then there is the possibility of dwelling hopefully in the borderlands of contemporary technoculture. If human beings, bearers of the *imago Dei*, are indeed 'natural-born cyborgs' then the twin narratives of apprehension and hope can aid in securing hybrid identity, leading to human agency that is just, compassionate and humble before God. In doing so, there is a very real possibility of living as 'image-bearing cyborgs'.

Torn between Body and Soul: the Evolved Body in Theological Perspective

Nicola Hoggard Creegan

Nicola Hoggard Creegan
Laidlaw College, Auckland, New Zealand

> It is no small pity, and should cause us no little shame, that, through our own fault, we do not understand ourselves... We know only that we are living in these bodies and have a vague idea, because we have heard it, and because our faith tells us so, that we possess souls. As to what good qualities there may be in our souls, or who dwells within them, or how precious they are, those are things which we seldom consider and so we trouble little about carefully preserving the soul's beauty.
> – Teresa of Avila, [1]

Teresa of Avila is right of course. But this does not mean that we value our bodies, or think much of whence they have come. Humans live uneasily, hovering between the world of animals and a world transcending this, determined in some cases to live as though we belong to neither realm— gods of our selves, and superior and dominating of the animals who have at times been seen as mere machines. Humans are restless creatures, constantly bewailing our bodies, frustrated by the limit of bodies, inspired by nonphysical and complex abstract and spiritual realities that transcend the body. We are observers of ourselves, and this distance propels us out

---

1. Theresa of Avila, *Interior Castle* (London: Thomas Baker, 1921), 39.

of our bodies, giving us a giddy but false sense of emancipation from material causality. Although many of us believe—both Christians and others—that we survive death, nevertheless we do not welcome death on the whole, and our activity here must always be via the body.

Indeed Reinhold Niebuhr refers to this paradoxical ambivalence of humanity, and the difficulty humans have when they attempt to define themselves too much in terms of their rationality and transcendence—forgetting anxiously their animal natures, or on the contrary forget their spiritual nature and indulge only in animal passions. These he defines as the two cardinal sins of humanity—the one pride, and other a form of hedonism or sensuality. In pride the human denies the limits of the body and of other life; in sensuality the person gives in to anxiety and denies all responsibility. Of the two sins, however it is pride that Niebuhr finds most common and most typical of the human condition.[2]

The thesis of this article is that whatever transcendent qualities of soul or intelligence or rationality we might possess we come to be that way via a long evolutionary progression; humans share a bodily make up with animals, we share a genetic and biochemical environment with them; we share complex social lives with the twenty or more hominid species which preceded us and the primate communities still struggling to survive in remote areas. This realisation of our long and very bodily emergence can lead us to despair at how material and physical and embodied we are, or it can give us a fresh perspective on our uniqueness and yet interconnectedness with the cosmos and other life—and a new view of our biblical role of dominion over other life. Human embodiment can be understood as being a means by which mediation is possible between the seen and the unseen because as humans we can speak of both, of the spiritual and the animal because we participate in both, and of the cosmic and the terrestrial because humans can know and imagine the very small and very large. Embodiment also gives us new clues to proper ways of knowing, and new insights into previously held political and theological doctrines.

---

2. Reinhold Niebuhr, *The Nature and Destiny of Man*, volume 1 (Louisville, Ky: Westminster/John Knox, 1996/1941), 178f.

1. Scientific reasons for emphasising our hominid and mammalian roots

MacIntrye has described our human embodiment this way:

> It is not just that our bodies are animal bodies with the identities and continuities of animal bodies . . . human identity is primarily, even if not only, bodily and therefore animal identity and it is by reference to that identity that the continuities of our relationships to others are partly defined.[3]

As MacIntyre argues, evidence is now mounting in all scientific disciplines for our close kinship with animals. Where previously we may have seen ourselves as more different than the same, the balance has now been shifted in the other direction. This new understanding, however, works both ways—we are not just the result of animals rewired; rather animals are more intelligent and more sentient than we once knew, and matter and life are more capable of bearing consciousness than we once supposed.

First, the evidence comes from the human genome. Clearly some scientists were expecting a much larger human genome and one more radically different from other animals.[4] Surprisingly we are, as is well known, genetically ninety-five to ninety eight percent the same as chimpanzees. We now know that small changes in DNA can have large effects on the organism, or even result in speciation.[5] Nevertheless the post-human genome view of the world is of DNA that is largely common to all similar species. No wide gap of information separates us from our primate cousins, though we must be careful how we interpret this and be mindful of the limits of our abilities to understand the human genome in its entirety.

DNA is not everything by any means, but we are increasingly aware that the same coding mechanism is used to make us that make other mammals and primates—and indeed all life. Rather than additions to our DNA

---

3. Alasdair C MacIntyre, *Dependent Rational Animals* (Peru, Illinois: Open Court, 1999), 40
4. Kate Bendall, 'Genes, the Genome and Disease', *New Scientist*, Feb 17 (2001), online: http://www.newscientist.com/article/mg16922787.200-genes-the-genome-and-disease.html?full=true.
5. Katherine S Pollard, 'What Makes Us Human?' *Scientific American,* May (2009): 32–37, 35.

there has been a reconfiguring of previous genes, with the slow addition of new information as insertions of jumping genes and viruses, or fusions and translocations of genetic material.[6] The HAR1 gene, for instance, is one of the genes that has undergone selective pressure since the time of the common ancestor. Yet this gene in some form was always a part of the genetic landscape.[7] Graeme Finlay has given us a fascinating glimpse of genetic similarities amongst great apes, including ourselves, and of the way evolution works at this level.[8] In *Homo divinus* and other articles Finlay has plotted the insertions of fragments, viruses and jumping genes into the family tree of primates and mammals at different points. In a method analogous to that of biblical text criticism these insertions can be used to plot the lineage of humans from great apes, and down even further into the mammalian line.

This has given us a great deal to think about. The issue of teleology has again been raised by some scientists reflecting on their work. Simon Conway Morris is one who has seen the ubiquity of evolutionary convergence as being suggestive of *telos*; if evolution repeatedly comes up with the same solutions like the camera eye again and again then some underlying direction or powerful 'constraint' is the most likely explanation. Thus evolution may be seen as prehending or anticipating what is to come.[9] Deep within the worm or the hominid or the primitive mammal more complex forms like humans were unpredictable possibilities, the substrate full of potential. Humans are connected with all other life and anticipated by it. Life is a more interconnected process than might once have been imagined.

Second, animal studies now show us that we are not athropomorphising when we ascribe emotions and indeed empathy to animals. Frans de Waal is one of many primatologists who have studied wild and captive populations of chimpanzees, and bonobos and has identified these emotions in primates. De Waal also studies these animals with an eye to how they can be interpreted in terms of human categories of morality and so-

---

6. But see also a dissenting view by Jeremy Taylor later in the chapter. Jeremy Taylor, *Not Chimps* (Oxford: Oxford University Press, 2009).
7. Pollard, 35.
8. Graeme Finlay 'Homo Divinus: The Ape that Bears God's Name', *Science and Christian Belief*, 15/1 (2003): 17–27.
9. The ubiquity of this phenomenon is described in Simon Conway Morris, *Life's Solution: Inevitable Humans in a Lonely Universe* (Cambridge: Cambridge University Press, 2003), 6.

cial organisation. De Waal argues: 'Being both more systematically brutal than chimps and more emphatic than bonobos, we are by far the most bipolar ape'.[10] He also names us the 'janus' ape, because 'we are the product of opposing forces, such as the need to think of our own interests and the need to get along'.[11]

De Waal notes that we have inherited both aggressive and deeply co-operative tendencies from our ape pre-cursors. In chimps, however, the aggression is kept more often in check by elaborate rituals of grooming and making up, and by close proximity. In humans these same tendencies become malicious and magnified; humans deal with much greater degrees of social isolation, and technology and language and intelligence vastly increases the lethality of our more vicious impulses.

De Waal observes the 'golden rule,' known by us as the rule that we should always treat others as we would like to be treated, operating in primate colonies and in communities of other animals like dolphins and elephants because these animals are able to put themselves in the position of another. Not only humans but primate communities also help those amongst them who are weak or crippled or intellectually handicapped.[12] Moreover, even the most hierarchical chimp community is flatter—if more conspicuously structured—than our contemporary societies are, making them more aware of another's need.[13] The golden rule is something we have also made more conscious and religious, and it is enshrined in the code of most religions.

The care of one another, the awareness of the other's need, and the keeping of social order by means of a stratified social group all highlight the way in which peculiarly human moral capacities have emerged out of a substratum of basic animal and biological behavior. In peculiarly human sentience and language we have brought uniqueness from this substratum. It is always possible to see human heights of legal and philosophical and moral thinking as utterly unique; at the same time it is also possible to appreciate the way in which human moral capacities have grown out of these pre-literate capacities, which are endemic in so called lower ani-

---

10. Frans De Waal, *The Inner Ape: The Best and Worst of Human Nature* (London: Granta, 2005), 221.
11. De Waal, *The Inner Ape*, 220.
12. De Waal, *The Inner Ape, 170.*
13. De Waal, *The Inner Ape,* 60–61.

mals. These observations allow us certainly to adjudicate once and for all on some social theories. There never was any such thing as the inherently lone individual bonding together with others in a 'social contract', for instance. Humans did not invent the social dimension; this is a part of our biological inheritance; the social accompanies embodiment for almost all animals. Most animals from ants to primates have a high degree of social interaction, the odd lone species notwithstanding.

Theologically this bodily social capacity should make the idea of a trinitarian God less arbitrary and abstract. How odd it would have been of this God to make in God's image essentially lone individuals. Moreover, although we are instructed to love as Christ loves us, this agape love has lower intimations in the cooperation and care found in all levels of living communities. Agape in its stringent demands may have been alien, but the direction it requires was embedded in the evolutionary progression from primitive creatures. And this should not be surprising, for the same Word who became flesh also is the one in whom 'all things hold together' (Col 1:17). and 'by whom all things were created' (Col 1:16). The human problem has always been in seeing and acknowledging this love that binds the world of matter together. Even in biology these findings are relevant. The idea of the 'selfish gene,' and of nature only 'red in tooth and claw' becomes a misleading simplification of the reality of co-operative life forms at all levels from that of the amoeba to that of the human. Humans are more tempted to self interest than are other life forms, but the capacity and the predilection for altruism is a part of primate and mammalian life.[14]

Third, the discovery of mirror neurons gives another objective backing to the thesis that humans and non-human animals participate alike in networks and communities of care and concern. These neurons make possible in the observer an experience analogous to that being observed in a fellow creature. Mirror neurons are common in all mammals and they help to make sense of the empathy we feel for animals, and they for us.[15]

---

14. Heterodoxy in evolutionary theory and in particular the ubiquity of cooperation is discussed in Jan Sapp, *Genesis: The Evolution of Biology* (New York: Oxford University Press, 2003).
15. Jeremy Taylor points out that mirror neurons have been assumed by most scientists to exist in humans, though they have not been directly located in the way they have in other mammals. See Jeremy Taylor, *Not a Chimp*, 240.

They also make sense of the obvious web of caring and concern that surrounds an animal community much as it does a human one.[16]

There is a connection, says de Waal, between self recognition in a mirror and empathy.[17] Thus the highest of human emotions is not only shared by lower animals but is tied strongly to recognition of the bodily form as self. Where once empathy may have been seen as that which enabled the flight of the human from the bondage of the body it is just the reverse—rooted in deep evolutionary mechanisms by which life becomes possible in social groups. Empathy is that which makes all moral life function, all relationships and everything which truly differentiates us from clever rule bound machines.

Nevertheless there are limits to empathy. Some animals have been documented coming to the aid of the young of other species, but empathy tends to break down at the borders of tribes, as indeed it does with humans.[18] Slight differences in bodily makeup signal 'otherness' and can result in predation or aggression, especially in chimp colonies, where other monkeys are often used as food in violent ways, chimps having a similar mix of cooperation and aggression as humans do.[19] Even between chimp colonies the borders of one tribe's territory are patrolled vigorously, though this is not so much the case for bonobos. We should not find it surprising, then, that humans are also predisposed to aggression—as well as care. Overcoming these body-linked prejudices does not come naturally; rather it requires recognition of their deep evolutionary roots, and their links to subtle differences in bodily make-up.

Fourth, even at the level of our chemical nature there are surprises. The chemicals that make our bodies are special, visible matter being only a very small amount of the matter of in the universe, and all visible matter apart from helium and hydrogen being born by nuclear combustion in the heart of stars many billions of years ago. (Dark energy and dark matter constitute perhaps ninety-six per cent of the mass of the universe.) Thus carbon, for instance, the building block of all animal existence is special, and carefully and wonderfully made, even if we take it for granted in our daily lives. That we share these scarce elements with all other forms of life,

---

16. De Waal, *The Inner Ape*, 177.
17. De Waal, *The Inner Ape*, 185.
18. De Waal, *The Inner Ape*, 137.
19. De Waal, *The Inner Ape*, 131.

along with the fragilities that this carbon based life imply, makes our kinship and connection to these forms more evident.[20] These constituents of bodiliness are a part of the wider story of our origins, a story we share with our primate cousins, and ultimately with all of life.

2. Emergence

These embodied realities raise questions about the architecture of our moral life together. Biological insights give us a great deal to think about when we consider human identity and the meaning of and the limits of *imago Dei* and dominion. We will return to these topics later in the article. But first I examine the issue of emergence, that process by which new more complex properties come out of a less complex substratum.[21] In strong theories of emergence it is postulated that these new phenomena are irreducible to and unpredictable at lower levels. An obvious example is the way in which carbon crystals take on new properties such as hardness and sparkle as diamond which are not properties of graphite, for instance. Any scientific appraisal of diamond must treat this level of being carbon as distinct from that of graphite. Weaker theories of emergence agree that more complex states exist but not that they are irreducible in theory. Either way emergence encourages us to see reality as layered and to respect the top down causality of the whole upon the part. Thus the discourse possible and appropriate at one level is no longer so at a higher level and vice versa.

Emergence is very evident at all levels of life; intelligence and personality emerge from the zygote even though the exact point at which these properties emerge is impossible to demarcate. Once emerged, however, intelligence has an profound downward effect upon the biology of an individual. In the evolutionary process humans can indeed be seen to have unique characteristics of wide ranging linguistically mediated intelligence

---

20. For a comprehensive telling of this story see Nancy Ellen Abrams & Joel Primack, *The View from the Center of the Universe: Discovering our Extraordinary Place in the Cosmos* (New York: Riverhead, 2006).
21. Philip Clayton and Paul Davies, ed, *The Re-Emergence of Emergence: The Emergentist Hypothesis from Science to Religion* (Oxford: Oxford University Press, 2006); Harold Morowitz, *The Emergence of Everything: How the World Became Complex* (Oxford: Oxford University Press, 2002); Robert B Laughlin, *A Different Universe: Reinventing Physics from the Bottom Down* (New York: Basic Books, 2005).

and imagination and these characteristics have lead in recent human history to our material and artistic culture and our highly developed moral and legal codes. The precursors of this uniqueness are evident in other mammals, corvids and dolphins but they have not passed a mysterious emergent line which makes us human. We are thus able to emphasise both the embodiment and animality of our human state, and at the same time to affirm that we appear to carry a unique development of earlier traits and ways of being.

Jeremy Taylor, however, in a recent book *Not A Chimp*, takes issue with what he sees as the opposite problem, the widespread conflating of the difference between humans and apes. He cites the statistics around percentage difference of DNA and argues that these are widely misleading because the gulf which separates us from chimps includes changes in gene expression related to the brain in particular, in which similar genes are turned on to a much higher degree than they were in previous species; humans also have hot-spots which are associated with 'rapid changes in mutation' and 'major increases in gene expression.'[22] He notes many instances of gene inversions and translocations which all amount to a great deal more change than the 2-3% often touted. Taylor also emphasises the discontinuities involved in language and material culture for instance, and argues that chimps cannot have human rights because they have no way of being held accountable for their actions.[23] All of this is true and is especially relevant in a world that does not recognise dominion or human uniqueness. Religious people, however, still more often have the opposite problem; they widen the gulf between chimp and human rather than conflating the two as Taylor has argued.[24]

What we are and our uniqueness must be recognised theologically as bound to an evolutionary progression, albeit an emergent one. Yet that progression always had within it the capacity to produce us, and the ani-

---

22. Jeremy Taylor, *Not a Chimp*, 124.
23. Jeremy Taylor, *Not a Chimp*, 307.
24. This may well be the first instance of a reaction against the 'humans are almost chimps' movement. Theologically, however, what Taylor says only further emphasises the deep connections we have with our chimp/human forbear. Only gene expression and gene translocation and inversion together with a small number of mutations separate us from them. Although this is quantitatively a much greater separation than a mere 2% it further underscores the sameness of the basic recipe in a way that Christians have not always understood in the past.

mals possess latent forms of characteristics like morality and language that nevertheless make us special. Not that any animals should be seen as merely a stage on the way to being human; they all possess their own ways of being and their own special character. More than souls longing to escape to the spiritual realm we are embodied but emergent persons linked inescapably to every level of our cosmic and biological evolutionary past. Thus in emphasising our animal inheritance it is imperative that we maintain this position within the context of the theory of emergence which allows that the genuinely new nevertheless comes to be, and that this emphasis be balanced by a proper understanding of our differences from other primate forms as well.

3. Scriptural perspectives on humans embodiment and distinctiveness

Whatever science says, is it not the case that Scripture emphasises only human uniqueness and the non-bodily aspects of our existence? Is Scripture not more interested in humans than in animals and their bodies? In previous centuries we could take our special nature for granted, coded in the doctrine of the *imago Dei,* and stemming often from an ignorance of the emotional life of animals. It was as though we had been delivered, as indeed some Christian still believe, straight from God, without evolutionary mediation. Even when evolution was allowed many believed that a second miracle of intervention occurred, essentially making us a special creation. Physically, anthropologically, genetically this boundary is now suspect, though it still exists as an emergent line. Our special character must be seen as a new but emergent reality, a mediating calling, linking the divine and the animal, linking the creation with the spiritual world around us, but not taking us out of or lifting us above that world in a way that emancipates us from the material.

What then does the Bible say about other life? Although the Bible is written by humans and about humans animals are raised in common and surprising ways. The creation of humans and animals occurs on the same figurative day (Gen 1:24–26), implying a linkage and a solidarity humans have not always been willing to admit; we have in the past instead emphasised the other side of this story—our image, our special creation from clay, and naming of and dominion over the animals. In the early chapters of Genesis a boat saves human and animal alike from drowning (Gen 6-7); God has directed that all life be saved. Solidarity is further emphasised by the similar fate under the angel of death in Egypt-the first born of both human and animal died (Ex 12:29). The fleeting images of restoration we are given in the prophets predict peace among the animals as much as in human society: 'the wolf will live with the lamb, the leopard will lie down with the goat, the calf and the lion and the yearling together; and a little child will lead them' (Isa 11:6), and 'the lion will eat straw like the ox . . . They will neither harm nor destroy on all my holy mountain' (Isa 65:25). Images of animal life abound, and are expressive of the inner spiritual life of emancipations and freedom. 'Then will the lame leap like a deer' (Isa 35:6) and, says the Lord, 'you will go out and leap like calves released from the stall' (Mal 4:1).

Jesus was born not in a place of high human culture, protected from the rest of creation, but in the midst of farm animals. A donkey bears his mother to Bethlehem (Mt 21:5) and Jesus to Jerusalem. In an enigmatic passage Jesus is said to have been ministered to by the wild animals in the desert when he endures his desert temptation (Mark 1:13). Jesus promises that God knows when a sparrow falls (Mt 10:29). Lambs will forever be associated with Christ himself, and in an especially telling phrase even the behaviour of the lamb and of the Saviour are compared: 'As a lamb before its shearers is silent' (Isa 53:7). All of these images are more consistent with a God who is intimately present to and caring of the whole of embodied creation than it is with a narrative of salvation for humans alone, and an emancipation eventually from all embodiment.

Moreover, Scripture shows a tendency to universalise and extend the circle of salvation. In Genesis Abraham is given a vision of all nations being blessed by his seed, but for much of the Old Testament the emphasis is on the small nation of Israel alone. Only the role of outsiders in the Scriptural story—a Pharaoh, Rahab, Ruth, a Persian King, the Roman Centurion at the crucifixion, and Ethiopian Eunuch—to name a few—give hints of what was discovered by the prophets of the universal intentions of God's love and salvation. Indeed in the New Testament Peter and Paul were initially at odds on the issue of the universality of the gospel (Gal 2:11-14). Similarly, it is consistent with biblical principles to press the circle of care and salvation far from our own xenophobic centre of concern. God's intention to redeem the whole creation is mentioned as hints emerging from the gospel miracles, the calming of the sea, (Matt 8:23–27) the healing of illness, the turning of water into wine (John 2:1–10); this redemption is also evident in the famous redemption passages of Colossians 1 and Romans 8. In eco-theology the circle has been extended and universalised to include all of creation in full measure, including sentient animals. It has been our ecological consciousness and the growing knowledge we have of animals that has led us in this direction and given us reason to think again about our own animal nature and embodiment.

4. Human distinctiveness

What of the Scriptural marker of distinction—the image of God, and mandate of dominion (Gen 1:28)? A great deal has been written about this gift or mandate to dominion mentioned in Genesis. What does it mean? For much of human history the logic of this story from Genesis has been used to justify human arrogance and the treatment of animals as other, or metaphysically different and lower.

Imago Dei has been a code word separating ourselves from the animals we exploit. In film we see this depicted most vividly in *Dances with Wolves*. A group of American Indians comes across a slaughter of buffalo and a clash of culture and of attitudes towards animals is vividly portrayed. The Indian would kill the buffalo for food, but respectfully, and always accompanied by thanks for the giving up of life of a fellow creature. Never were they slaughtered for game. We now know that all human societies altered their landscape and the flora and fauna within it. Maori apparently decimated the Moa population,[25] for instance, but a new level of destruction accompanied the white political/Christian domination of the globe, not because Christians were misinterpreting Genesis, but because the story of dominion did little to restrain human excess, and seemed to justify them.

And it is only as we contemplate our own embodiment and the long history of our pre-human embodiment that dominion makes sense. It is *because* we share with animals so much of our neural and biochemical apparatus–and we now know our genetic material—that we can act as agents of dominion. If we come with other assumptions, of metaphysical 'other-

---

25. This point is controversial and rats undoubtedly also contributed, but is discussed in Philippa Mein Smith, *A Concise History of New Zealand* (Cambridge/Melbourne: Cambridge University Press, 2005), 14.

ness' for instance, the risk of harsh, utilitarian and inhumane treatment becomes amplified—as has been the case in the past.

Dominion as it perhaps should be is present in apocryphal tales of the work of St Francis who is said to have tamed the wild wolf. Farmers though the centuries have cared for their animals and pastures. In the technological age, however, caring dominion has been rare. It is exemplified brilliantly in a story from the *Life of Pi*.[26] The author, Yann Martel, the winner of Booker Prize in 2002, tells the story of a young boy, a zoo keeper's son from India, who is marooned for 277 days on a 26 foot life boat with a live Bengali tiger, a hyena, a zebra and an orangutan.

The hyena, the zebra and the orangutan eat one another or are eaten by the tiger. Only the boy, Pi, is left, along with the tiger. Before he leaves on this ill fated journey the reader finds out that he is a very religious child, so religious that he believes in Christianity, Hinduism and Islam, the more ways of worshipping God the better. In this mystical story the child wins over the live Bengali tiger. He tames him. Pi becomes the alpha male on this little boat. If ever there were a description of taming of the wild creatures it is this, in the delicate peace fought for and won on this little boat. Boy and tiger pitted against each other. Boy taming tiger because he knows him well, because they both recognise the same cellular and bodily signals, and because at heart Pi loves his animals.

Where contemporary theology might differ from the theology of the past might be in locating the power of dominion in our common ancestry and solidarity and not only in an endowed special quality of image. Humans do rule the animals and the plants, but humans are embedded within, incarnate within the animal and plant kingdoms.

Christopher Southgate, for instance, in his recent book *The Groaning*, argues that the evolutionary process is necessarily ambiguous, being both full of value and apparent disvalue in the suffering and extinction of creatures.[27] Nevertheless humans have a position or calling to help heal the creation, to use their special freedom to mediate as priests and co-creators with God. Going beyond the normal understanding of stewardship, he argues that humans being both the product of evolution but also rising above it in our special ability to transcend the process of selving, or becoming a self, are to 'be part . . . of transforming the world, making it more

---

26. Yann Martel, *Life of Pi* (Orlando: Harcourt, 2001).
27. Southgate, *The Groaning of Creation*, (Westminster/John Knox, 2008), 94.

than it is currently is, starting to help to heal its ambiguity and travail.'[28] This requires that we attend to creation as it truly is, and have a self sacrificing relationship to the creation, not seeking to exist at the expense of other creatures, but instead living our pivotal roles in the service of creation, enabling creatures to flourish where previously they might have been thwarted.

Nevertheless humans are different from animals, not just in our dominion, but in our abilities for abstract communication and the building of material culture. We can see to the ends of the universe, to the beginnings of time; we can imagine worlds that do not exist and feast on abstract number systems with no known physical correlations. What makes us different is now an urgent problem in both science and theology. J Wentzel Van Huyssteen takes up this task in his Gifford Lectures and book, *Alone in the World?* He argues both for our uniqueness and for our animality:

> contemporary scientists have successfully argued for . . . the animality of our humanity . . . The fascinating result of this research was that both the break between humans and the great apes, and the separation of races from one another were thus diminished, while at the same time human uniqueness was ever more carefully defined.[29]

This is the conclusion that we might expect for a creature which has emerged out of the evolutionary process. Thus even in wishing to argue for difference it is the continuities that also matter. Van Huyssteen argues that it is the opening up of the capacities of the human brain that gives our minds the fluidity and far reaching qualities, the self reflective qualities that can finally be called sentience and self consciousness and that invite and encourage the highest moral and intellectual capacities. Even these highest qualities are products of our embodiment, and of our evolutionary progression. This knowledge, says MacIntrye, is crucial to our moral development. If we ignore our embodiment, seeing it as 'contingent and external' we also ignore the virtues of dependency and compassion that

---

28. Southgate, *The Groaning*, 103.
29. J Wentzel Van Huyssteen, *Alone in the World: Human Uniqueness in Science and Theology* (Grand Rapids: Eerdmans, 2006), 52.

are entailed by and required of this embodied human condition.[30] MacIntyre goes on to draw further parallels between our kinship to animals, our sharing with them in 'forms of life' and yet our being unique in other aspects of our development and life as in our language use.[31]

5. Theological implications of evolutionary embodiment

Evolutionary embodiment, then, can give us better insights into how we should take dominion, and the sense in which our *imago Dei* has been anticipated in lower life forms. This should come as no theological surprise; and emphasis on continuities as well as discontinuities has long characterised theological discourse.

Evolutionary embodiment can also give us insights about human knowing, and it can be a proper chastening of the human pride of which Niebuhr speaks. A surprising amount of communication and communal living at a complex level takes place in primate communities without the help of language as we know it, including the very vital knowledge of how other individuals are feeling. This should give us new insight into the metaphor of 'indwelling' associated with human knowing. For even animals know this way: 'We have seen that the exhilaration shown by apes and babies' says Polanyi, 'when solving a problem prefigures the intellectual joys of science'.[32]

Those capacities we might once have associated strictly with our human minds and their capacities to venture beyond the body and to be emancipated from it are now linked vitally to pre-human communities. Human knowing, then, for all its transcendent heights, is linked inevitably to the knowing through the body at which primates, and also elephants and dolphins and corvids have become so skilled. The body is not the vehicle waiting to give birth to the human mind which can then be emancipated from its origins. These origins give us a clue to our common life and the life of the mind. This makes sense of Polanyi's insistence that it is 'fiduciary trust' and not 'doubt' that most characterises true human know-

---

30. MacIntyre, *Dependent Rational Animals*, 50.
31. MacIntyre, Dependent Rational Animals, 58.
32. Michael Polanyi, *Personal Knowledge: Towards a Post-Critical Philosophy* (Chicago: University of Chicago Press, 1974) 194.

ing. Even with tools, he claims, 'we pour ourselves into them and assimilate them'[33] so that they too become parts of the body.

Knowledge by indwelling is immensely important for religious knowing. Van Huyssteen explains that ever since humans left traces of material culture in the Upper Paleolithic, on the caves of France and Spain we were also deeply religious. The mind which had been given birth in an ancient brain was aware of transcendent and hidden realities. He argues that this 'evolutionary epistemology' is more likely to be trusted than otherwise.[34]

Evolutionary embodiment can be a reason for despair and for a sense that everything that appears transcendent is really only material. Properly understood, however, our embodiment is reason to see humans as standing in an important place of mediation, and that this mediation might itself be a clue to the mysteries of the soul about which Theresa of Avila speaks. In the human mind, and perhaps nowhere else on earth, the physical material matter of which we are made is able to grasp the eternal. We of all creatures, as Schleiermacher says, see 'all finite things in and through the infinite.'[35] In dominion we have the possibility of mirroring this transcendence back into the animal world. Human powers are in a sense godlike vis-à-vis the natural and especially the animal world; such powers are seen in the human ability to control and manipulate the natural world and therefore the lifeworld of animals, and humans also have a power of life and death over animals, a power to care and to tyrannise even the most gifted of other creatures.

5. Conclusion

Human embodiment, then, is understood as crucial to all that makes us unique as well as everything that links us to the animal world we inhabit. Our higher powers come from animal pre-cursors and are not liberated from them. Human moral life is built upon the strengths and weaknesses of the primate animals who preceded us and with whom we still share habitat. Ever since the human animal emerged other animals are increasingly affected by our existence for good or for ill. Yet the biblical mandate

---

33. Michael Polanyi, *Personal Knowledge*, 59.
34. Van Huyssteen, *Alone in the World?*, 77.
35. Friedrich Schleiermacher, *On Religion: Speeches to its Cultured Despisers*, trans. Terrence N Tice (Richmond, Va: John Knox, 1969), 79.

to dominion should make this relationship one of mutual dependency and appreciation. The story humans can tell of origins in the distant evolutionary past is also the story of our animal cousins. This crucial embodiment gives us insight into our ways of knowing, and our calling. Rather than conjuring up a shallow materialism this vision and story of embodiment are reason to see humanity as playing a crucial role in mediating various aspects of cosmic and earthly reality.

Young People, Technoculture and Embodied Spirituality

Craig Mitchell

Craig Mitchell
Uniting College for Leadership and Theology, Adelaide, Australia

> 'I blog, therefore I am.'
> Giles Turnbull[1]

> '... if you want to account for a people, look at their young.'
> Kenda Creasy Dean[2]

Any parent will tell you that the lives of their children have been seduced by technology, with endless texting, chatting, gaming, and surfing. Family households dedicate increasing hours and income to information and communication technologies (ICT). Although it is easy to think of technology as mechanical and therefore inhuman, increasingly, ICT is not only 'intelligent' but also inseparable from human behaviours and attitudes. A new study of 2000 US teenagers indicates that their media use is increasing (currently 7½ hours per day), along with their propensity to 'multi-task' (twenty-nine percent of their media time).[3] The daily existence of the vast majority of young people is enmeshed in technoculture.

---

1. Giles Turnbull, 'I Blog, Therefore I Am', BBC News. http://news.bbc.co.uk/2/hi/in_depth/sci_tech/2000/dot_life/1799998.stm, 2002. Accessed 28 May, 2009
2. Kenda Creasy Dean, *Practicing Passion: Youth and the Quest for a Passionate Church* (Grand Rapids: Eerdmans, 2004), 11.
3. Victoria Rideout, Ulla Foehr, and Donald Roberts, *Generation M²: Media in the Lives of 8- to 18-Year Olds* (Menlo Park CA: Kaiser Foundation, 2010). http://www.kff.org/

This article suggests that current research regarding the spirituality of young people gives insufficient attention to the place of technology in their lives. Young peoples' innate desires for intimacy and self-transcendence are bound up in their daily use of technology. These spiritual yearnings are embodied insofar as they are located within, rather than in opposition to, adolescents' physiological and psycho-social development, and are further embodied in their personal media practices or habits.

The body has long been a significant theme in relation to the wellbeing of young people, both in practical theology and in the broader social sciences: indeed, it remains a lens through which their lives and loves are viewed and judged. Rather than seeing in teenagers' media use the desire for physical or psychological escape from the world, we might instead recognise their longings for connectedness and meaningful self-expression.

The promises and perils of technology mirror some of the perceived risks often associated with puberty. Within technoculure, both sexuality and spirituality co-exist as mediated dimensions of the lives of teenagers. The quests for bodily intimacy and self-transcendence find particular expression in technological practices. The suggestion here is that the negative views and concerns of church and society towards technology in the lives of young people parallel attitudes regarding adolescent sexuality. In this regard, 'cyber' is the new 'sex'. To understand this situation requires an examination of both current and historical views regarding teenage spirituality, sexuality and the body.

1. Studying the Spirituality of Generation Y

Recent studies of the spirituality of young people, both in Australia and overseas, recognise the social dimensions of spiritual experience, yet give little attention to the interplay between technology and spirituality. While acknowledging the significance of media use, researchers have not sufficiently examined the social uses of technology as possible arenas for spiritual experience.

The connection between spiritual development and social engagement is a recurring theme in studies of youth and young adults.[4] According to

---

entmedia/mh012010pkg.cfm. Accessed 31 January 2010.
4. While 'spirituality' and 'faith' are not synonymous, Fowler's universal notion of faith is seen here as having correspondence with an understanding that all human beings

the international, multi-faith research by the Search Institute's *Centre for Spiritual Development*, spiritual development has three dimensions:[5]

- connecting and belonging
- becoming aware of or awakened to self and life
- developing a way of living

In this schema, relational connectedness is a necessary aspect of healthy spirituality, both in terms of a sense of the transcendent or divine and of interdependence with other people. The outward capacity for mature relationship with others and the world correlates with the inward capacity to experience awe, wonder and mystery. Erik Erikson recognised decades ago that the capacity for mature intimacy requires growth beyond the egocentrism of adolescence.[6] James Fowler, building on Erikson, identified a similar developmental need for faith to grow beyond peer-influenced certainty.[7] His Stage Four in faith development described a more individualised, reflexive stance, able to see from another's perspective, and hence, more open to diverse viewpoints, while the aforementioned Search Institute study affirms that in terms of spirituality, healthy psychological development relates to relational wellbeing.

Australian research recognises the importance of the social world of young people, yet defines spirituality quite differently. The *Spirit of Generation Y* study constitutes the most comprehensive study of adolescent spirituality undertaken in Australia to date. Sponsored primarily by mainline churches and church schools, the study used multiple research methods across a range of audiences. The study's researchers differed over the method of interpreting the findings, the result being two reports, *Putting Life Together* by Hughes and *The Spirit of Generation Y* by Mason, Singleton and Webber.[8]

---

have spiritual awareness by virtue of being human. See James Fowler, *Stages of Faith* (San Francisco: HarperOne, 1995).
5. Eugene Roehlkepartain *et al*, *With Their Own Voices* (Minneapolis: Search Institute, 2008).
6. Erik Erikson, *Childhood and Society* (New York: Norton, 1963).
7. Fowler, *Stages of Faith*.
8. Philip Hughes, *Putting Life Together* (Fairfield: Fairfield Press/Christian Research Association, 2007); Michael Mason, Andrew Singleton and Ruth Webber, *The Spirit of Generation Y* (Mulgrave: John Garratt Publishing, 2007).

For Hughes, spirituality represents the higher part of a person's nature, that which causes us to go beyond everyday ethical expectations, where true self-giving, compassion and awareness of the divine occur. Negative attitudes and actions are at odds with the spiritual. Hence not all people are spiritual; rather it is a state of awareness and agency to which we might aspire.

The Spirit of Generation Y defines spirituality quite differently as 'a conscious way of life based on a transcendent referent'.[9] Spirituality requires a particular choice of a worldview and ethos with which to adhere. Hence the authors test what kind of difference the adoption of a particular worldview (Christian, Buddhist, New Age, etc) makes to a young person's values and attitudes. Once again, not all people are spiritual by this definition, and different systems of spirituality can be compared. One can see the attraction of both approaches for the churches and Christian schools sponsoring the joint study.

The above two understandings are at odds with James Fowler's theory that all human beings have faith, and that what differs among us is the object of our faith and its level of maturity. Hughes' view also differs from a Jungian perspective that sees evidence of the spiritual in the dark side of human nature. In *Virtual Faith*, Tom Beaudoin hears in bleak and brooding rock music the spiritual yearnings of young people.[10] For David Tacey the adolescent preoccupation with death and evil is evidence of an innate spiritual quest for a rite of passage to adulthood.[11] My critique of the Hughes and Mason studies is that their limited definitions of spirituality fail to attend to the ways in which young people might seek spiritual experiences or construct spiritual meaning other than through exemplary ethical aspirations or coherent belief systems.

Secondly, in defining spirituality in terms of peace, happiness, intelligibility and meaning, the studies not only impose seemingly adult notions of spirituality on young people, they also fail to explore sufficiently the place of risk, adventure, and other liminal bodily experiences. Hughes' identification of the importance of excitement scratches at the surface

---

9. *Ibid*, 39.
10. Tom Beaudoin, *Virtual Faith* (San Francisco: Jossey-Bass, 1998).
11. David Tacey, 'Authenticity and Spirituality', in *Proceedings from Exploring Adolescent Spirituality* (Melbourne: Centre for Adolescent Health, University of Melbourne, 1997).

of deeper questions. At a spirituality research seminar that I attended in the US in 2008, one researcher commented that after an interview with a young man about spirituality, the interviewee said, 'I wasn't going to say this in the interview, but I feel the most spiritual when I'm having sex with my girlfriend'. This illustrates the difficulty of researchers exploring aspects of spirituality relating to intimacy and the body with young people, especially where the research contexts are clearly religious, such as in a church school.

This issue overlaps with investigation of technology use as an arena in which sexuality, intimacy and spirituality may be inter-related. *The Spirit of Generation Y* report recognised the significance of technology in the lives of young people, particularly their use of mobile phones and the Internet. 'This involves new ways of communicating, alternative ways of managing relationships and new spaces in which friendships are conducted.'[12] The study analysed 'screen time' per week and discussed TV and film viewing with young people. In terms of whether media culture causes young people to adhere to non-traditional spiritual beliefs (such as 'New Age'), the authors concluded that 'popular culture is more about entertainment first, then perhaps is used to assist in personal expression. It does not constitute a major influence on spirituality, values or world-views.'[13] According to these authors, media have little influence on young people's adherence to coherent religious systems. Hughes confirms the importance of music across the thirteen to twenty-four year age range as being the most important aid to achieving peace and happiness. Otherwise, *Putting Life Together* contains limited discussion of technology.

Both studies analyse ICT largely as transmission media rather than as avenues for social interaction. While recognising the social dimensions of technology use, neither study gives particular attention to exploring whether technology-enabled intimacy produces self-knowledge or self-transcendence in ways that are spiritually significant for young people. Furthermore, these studies have not investigated the extent to which the sexual development of the young person may of itself involve a profound spiritual quest toward mature adulthood. At the heart of the problem are the ambivalent views of church and society towards the bodies and bodily development of young people. I suggest that in fact the two issues stated

---

12. Michael Mason *et al*, *The Spirit of Generation Y*, 239
13. *Ibid*, 247.

here are related, namely the possibility of technology use being spiritually significant and the problem of technology being seen as an area of sexual risk.

2. Adolescence: The body revolution

Throughout the last century, definitions and representations of adolescence have often centred on the body. The modern notion of 'youth' initially focused on the physiological changes that accompany puberty. Stanley Hall's classic definition of adolescence in the early 1900s centred on youth as a time of biological transformation.[14] According to Hall, in adolescence a person underwent an evolutionary process, morphing from primate to modern adult. This transition was both physical and psychological, a change in mind, body and consciousness; hence the emergence of more than just reproductive capability. The development of the human being from childhood through adolescence to adulthood consisted of a necessary recapitulation of the journey from savage to citizen.

Thus emerged the notion of youth as barbarians who needed civilising, an idea that shaped social science and social work, including education, health care, youth clubs (including church youth work), social work, and juvenile justice. While Hall and those who influenced him saw the terrors of the teenage years as a positive dimension of normal human development, the perceived 'sturm und drang' (storm and stress) of adolescence became the rationale for western approaches to youth work that included political control, social exclusion and ideological indoctrination.

The physical and cognitive changes of adolescence require a cultural narrative that gives meaning to this turbulent passage from childhood to adulthood. Hall's legacy was that western society came to see in young people's idealism and imperfections the conflicted nature of humanity. While his theories no longer have currency, there seems little doubt that the 20th century marked an unprecedented focus on youth as icons and iconoclasts of social progress. Corporate culture managed to capitalise on both views. From as early as the 1930's, the parallel developments of social science, the mass media and consumer culture resulted in an eruption of financial and cultural activity centred on teenagers as, literally, the em-

---

14. G Stanley Hall, *Adolescence: Its Psychology and its Relations to Physiology, Anthropology, Sociology, Sex, Crime, Religion and Education* (London: Sydney Appleton, 1905).

bodiment of individual and national progress. Yet at the same time, young people's rebellious attitudes and actions personified the fears of parents, teachers, employers and politicians.

In the post-World War II years, social representations of youth have tended to idolise or demonise young people, portraying them as the embodiment of social ideals, including physical perfection, or alternatively as delinquents and vandals—rebels without a cause.[15] Australian research indicates that mass media over-represent young people's behaviour as delinquent or criminal.[16] Hence young people are to be seen on screen, billboard and magazine cover but not heard from in the public arena; allowed to compel and attract but not permitted to be distractive or disruptive.

Crawford and Rossiter speak of youth marketing as 'the marketing strategy of inadequacy'.[17] While we cannot solely blame the media for problems of youth, we must consider whether conflicting social expectations contribute to their low self-esteem, dissatisfaction with body image, eating disorders, risky behaviour and deliberate self-harm. A 2008 national survey of 45,600 young Australians aged eleven to twenty-four by Mission Australia identified drugs, stress and depression, body image and personal safety as four primary issues of teenage concern.[18] In another study:

> Mental disorders were the leading contributor to the burden of disease and injury (49%) among young Australians aged 15–24 years in 2003, with anxiety and depression being the leading specific cause for both males and females.[19]

---

15. For example, Christine Griffin, *Representations of Youth* (Cambridge: Blackwell, 1993).
16. Judith Bessant, Howard Sercombe and Rob Watts, *Youth Studies: An Australian Perspective* (Melbourne: Addison Wesley Longman, 1998).
17. Marissa Crawford and Graham Rossiter, *Reasons for Living* (Melbourne: ACER Press, 2006), 150.
18. Mission Australia, *National Survey of Young Australians* (Sydney: Mission Australia, 2008).
19. Australian Institute of Health and Welfare (AIHW), *Young Australians: Their Health and Wellbeing* (Canberra: AIHW, 2007), 23.

There is evidence that mass media representations of teenage bodies negatively affect adolescent self-image, particularly for girls.[20] A cursory examination of magazines in any newsstand reveals ample evidence that the body has a central place in social representations regarding the place, role and potential of teenagers. The social construction of adolescence places their bodily development within a conflicted cultural narrative in which expectation and reality are at odds, contributing to both physiological and psychological risk and dysfunction. The link between body image, wellbeing and mental health is suggestive of a spirituality strongly related to one's sense of self. The point here is not to establish psychological cause and effect, but to question the social and cultural story that shapes the identities of young people. Negativity regarding the developing body may result in dissociation between self-image and spiritual wellbeing. Rather than being 'embodied', such spirituality might be viewed as 'antibodied'. To what extent has the Christian church reflected such social and cultural narratives in its theology and ministry with young people?

3. Adolescence in Christian theology

The teenage body has been a significant theme in Christian youth ministry, with a similarly conflicted narrative. Until the last decade, Christian theology has given little explicit attention to adolescence, leaving denominational and para-church youth ministries to develop theologies-in-practice. Historically, denominational youth ministries of the nineteenth and early twentieth centuries included elements of instruction in the faith, wholesome recreation, leadership development, safe fellowship, worship, moral formation and recruitment for ministry.[21] These activities can be seen both as formative and protective, providing a secure haven within which to inculcate moral and spiritual values while shaping the next generation of leaders. We could describe such ministry with body metaphors of shelter, nurture and exercise.

---

20. Duane Hargreaves and Marika Tiggemann, 'Idealised media images and adolescent body image: "comparing boys and girls"'. *Body Image*, Volume 1 (2004), pp351-361;. Patricia van den Berg *et al*, 'Body dissatisfaction and body comparison with media images in males and females', *Body Image*, Volume 4 (2007), pp257-268.
21. Norman F Nelson, *To Help Them Find Their Feet* (Brisbane: Smith & Paterson, 1966) and C Irving Benson, *A Century of Victorian Methodism* (Melbourne: Spectator Publishing, 1935).

An emerging theme in twentieth century youth ministry was the perception that the physiological turmoil of puberty made young people particularly susceptible to sensual desires.

> Like the metal filings in the presence of a magnet, youth orient themselves toward a culture's peculiar seductions and align their desires with the most powerful force that seems to desire them.[22]

As adolescence became a more discrete social category, churches' reactions to the accompanying youth culture involved more recognition of the temptations and 'sins' of the flesh, particularly related to sex, drugs and lack of social self-control. Hall's early twentieth century theory of recapitulation, described above, was, in a sense, translated theologically into an inner, personal struggle with base bodily desires; young people must not only be taught the right way to live, but also set free from the sins that threaten their safe passage through puberty to mature adulthood. They must be emancipated not only socially but also spiritually. For the churches, spiritual wellbeing was seen to embody chaste living.

A key element of the post-World War II social revolution was the shift of sexuality from the private to the public sphere. Griffin notes that 'adolescence as a concept is distinctly sexualised', particularly in the social and medical sciences.[23] A similar locus of concern emerged in Christian youth ministry: the bodies of teenagers became individual battlegrounds between holiness and sinfulness, between sacred and secular, between church and world.[24] For example, I recall the youth worker who asked the girls in his youth group to imagine that everyone who touched them anywhere left an indelible fingerprint, and then asking how they would feel on their wedding night when their husband saw the blemishes of their past.[25]

However stark that example seems, in reality the contemporary social and theological narratives that correlate teenage bodies with imperfection and sinfulness are so pervasive as to be almost invisible. Advertising

---

22. Dean, *Practising Passion*, 30.
23. Griffin, *Representations of Youth*, 160.
24. For example, John C Souter, *Love* (Wheaton: Tyndale House, 1985).
25. At the time, the youth worker did not state whether or not boys were asked a similar question.

that idolises youth is designed as much as projection of adult desire as it is an appeal to adolescent dreams. In *Useless Beauty*, Robert Johnson sees the book of Ecclesiastes mirrored in the film *American Beauty*, where midlife crisis finds partnership with adolescent yearning for fulfillment.[26] If young people act out the longings of older generations, it is not surprising that their social beatification is more as Persephone, consort of the underworld than as Aphrodite, goddess of love. Adolescent sexuality, particularly female sexuality, is frequently portrayed in films as manipulative, the source of adult temptation and fall.[27] However the biblical narratives themselves are a sober reminder that it is the young who have often been exploited or preyed upon.[28]

What ministry metaphors portray teenagers as filled with sinful desire, needing to be separated from the world and cleansed before being redeemed? Not shelter, nurture and exercise but, perhaps, defense, denial, capitulation and release.

Churches in New Zealand and Australia were not uniformly judgmental of adolescent desires, and worked at ways of expressing more liberal theology through contemporary educational theory and practice. As a youth worker and author in the late 1980's and 1990's, I used and prepared resources concerning young people's identities, decision-making and behaviour, including their sexuality.[29] At the time, values clarification approaches were respectful of individual autonomy while attending to communal norms. However, such approaches usually left the adjudication of difference among peers abstracted from the wisdom of parents and grandparents. When it came to communicating about the body, teenagers and elders were rarely in the same room, let alone on the same page.

On the one hand, in the latter half of the twentieth century, mainline views in the churches seemed to correspond with broader social attitudes concerning the psychosocial development of young people, while nevertheless seeing popular youth culture as a threat to healthy development.

---

26. Robert K Johnston, *Useless Beauty* (Grand Rapids: Baker Academic, 2004).
27. See, for example, the movies *Thirteen*, *Election Day* and the aforementioned *American Beauty*.
28. For example, the Levite's concubine in Judges 19, the rape of Tamar in 2 Samuel 3, and Lot and his daughters in Genesis 19.
29. For example, Craig Mitchell, 'Let's Talk About Sex', *Top Gear: Discipleship Studies for Youth*, Volume 5 (1992): 16–27; and Michael Shimek, *Dating and Marriage* (Minneapolis: Winston Press, 1978).

Christian youth ministry provided a safe, spiritual fellowship as a healthy alternative to the sexualised youth culture. Both the group environment and firm leadership were seen as important in providing a necessary haven from temptation. Hence youth spirituality becomes strongly associated with safety, community and right behaviour. It is not difficult to see how these developments might contribute to a narrowing of the lens through which the spiritual lives of young people are viewed.

4. Passion, relationship and presence

In the past decade, some youth ministry authors reference the body in redefining ministry with young people, offering ways through and beyond these dilemmas. Kenda Creasy Dean, a prominent youth ministry theologian, suggests that adolescent development is a God-given gift to the world and to the church, rather than a suffering to be endured.[30]

> Although the brain's frontal lobes governing reasons and judgement continue to develop into adulthood, by adolescence the emotional centres of the brain are well on their way to maturity, giving teenagers their propensity for leading with their hearts. In other words, the adolescent brain is wired for passion . . .[31]

For Dean, such passion is the source of young people's raw idealism, a longing for intimacy and desire for significance—a cause worth living and dying for. While Dean doesn't deny the wild rollercoaster that is adolescence, she sees in human passions the imprint of divine passion, open to be redeemed rather than negated. In particular, God's fidelity, transcendence and communion engage and transform the adolescent's desire for steadfastness, ecstasy and immanence. Teenage passion is met by the pathos of God, the suffering love of Jesus Christ, whose saving work is to meet, complete and direct teenage desire. Dean's work paves the way for a theology that sees young people's physical development as not being at odds with their spiritual development.

---

30. Dean, *Practising Passion*.
31. *Ibid*, 6.

I suggest that such bodily themes move beyond both shelter and formation metaphors, and also guilt and submission, to suggest acceptance, presence, faithfulness, suffering and joy.

Andrew Root further critiques youth ministry and develops body themes of relationship and presence.[32] For over two decades, youth ministry in the Western world has been described as relational, more founded on friendship than on instruction or recreation. Root suggests that youth ministry, particularly among US evangelicals, used relationship as a carrot to attract young people into the programs and agendas of the church or ministry group. Such ministries described Jesus as a compassionate boundary-crossing leader, treating incarnation as a pattern for attractional ministry rather than as a theological foundation. Root suggests that these ministries were designed to exert personal influence on young people within a Christian cultural enclave. Their ministry success was demonstrated through charismatic leadership and multiple gatherings, large and small that could inculcate Christian identity, again associating spirituality with safe group environments.

Drawing on the theology of Dietrich Bonhoeffer, Root sees the Jesus Christ as the very incarnation of God; incarnation in youth ministry is not simply an attractional strategy.

> ... God's heart yearns to be near to humanity ... through the incarnation there is a direct solidarity between human being and human being made possible by the humanity of God in Christ.[33]

In seeing incarnation as inseparable from the Cross, Root's conclusion is that 'relational youth ministry is about suffering with adolescents', about place-sharing with young people on their terms rather than personal influence on our terms.[34] Real bodily presence with young people is at the heart of Christ-centred relationships. Other recent youth ministry writing expands related themes of presence and connectedness, in terms of

---

32. Andrew Root, *Revisiting Relational Youth Ministry* (Downers Grove: IVP Books, 2007).
33. *Ibid*, 89.
34. *Ibid*.

relational affinity,[35] faith-forming communal practices,[36] discipleship as shared pilgrimage[37] and spiritual disciplines that centre on the experience of God's presence.[38]

These writers seek to define ministry with young people as embodied, present, authentic and engaging. At the same time, they take seriously the need for the presence of a discipling community, participation in spiritual habits, and attentiveness to the young person as a person—someone to sit alongside for his or her own sake. The authors firstly call the church to focus youth ministry on the spiritual lives of young people, their experiences of the presence of the divine or sacred in their lives, and secondly, they commend Christian discipleship as a process that requires a community of presence and embodied practices. In contrast with previous approaches, vulnerability is emphasised over safety, and spirituality seen as requiring personal investment and discipline, not simply group participation.

What may be less evident is the extent to which these developments are both a reaction to the spread of technology and an attempt to engage with it. In attempting to redefine youth ministry, the above authors and others are in part responding to the social, cultural and economic revolution generated in the twentieth century through growth in information and communication technologies. Their call for presence, authenticity and discipleship practice seems in part an attempt to rescue young people from private worlds, virtual relationships and mediated experiences. One could go so far as to say that the tangible presence of the church, the body of Christ, represents a counter-cultural, immediate alternative to the mediated experiences provided by technoculture. While such authors view the body in more positive terms than their predecessors, the impact of technology upon young people is seen generally as problematic, and yet the relationship between the two is largely unexplored.

Dean's thesis invites a further reframing of the conversation. What if we were to see in young people's innate use of communicative technology

---

35. Mark Oestreicher, *Youth Ministry 3.0* (Grand Rapids: Zondervan/Youth Specialties, 2008).
36. Fred Edie, *Book, Bath, Table and Time* (Cleveland: Pilgrim Press, 2007).
37. *The Way of Pilgrimage* series (Nashville: Upper Room, 2007).
38. Mark Yaconelli, *Contemplative Youth Ministry* (Grand Rapids: Zondervan/Youth Specialties, 2006).

not a negative denial of their true needs, but in fact an authentic search for well-being, meaning and intimacy? Indeed, what if their communicative capacities, augmented by technology, are inseparable from this spiritual quest? The increasing embodiment of ICT suggests a high degree of integration of the self with both the means of communication and its subjects.

5. The embodiment of technology

> Young people, like technologies, are constructed within popular discourse as the natural inheritors of future societies, and young people's mastery of technologies is read as inevitable.[39]

Technology is so integrated within modern society that some authors now speak of 'technoculture'.[40] Rather than simply referring to electronics entangling everyday life, technoculture is defined as the ways in which in people value and use information and communication technologies 'in the mediated construction of culture'.[41] In other words, the application of technology is inter-related with its users' capacities for interpretation, invention and reinvention within the socio-cultural realm.

In my observation, certain technologies, in their design, functionality and actual usage, are increasingly 'embodied' in one or more of these ways:

- *minituarisation*—allowing physical portability and adding stylistic value;
- *personalisation*—technology styled as an individual fashion accessory that appears trendy or 'cool';
- *functionality*—increasingly complex functions are presented with apparently simple control and feedback mechanisms;
- *customisation*—features, controls and accessories can be varied by the user;
- *sensation*—increasingly sophisticated sensory and tactile control and feedback characteristics;

---

39. Keri Facer and Ruth Furlong, 'Beyond the myth of the "cyberkid": Young people at the margins of the information revolution', *Journal of Youth Studies*, Volume 4 Number 4 (2001): 452.
40. Lelia Green, *Technoculture: From Alphabet to Cybersex* (Sydney: Allen & Unwin, 2002).
41. *Ibid*, xxciii.

- *portability*—increasing capacity to function in a range of locations, including network access and capability
- *virtuality*—increasing capacity to portray life-like situations or fantasy situations with realistic or hyper-real characteristics;
- *multi-functionality*—through performing multiple functions, the likelihood of a single product (such as a mobile phone) being seen as indispensable increases, along with its style value (either recreational or commercial);
- *cost*—while some devices are not cheap by any means, they are priced to be seen as necessary accessories for various income brackets.

This list is not exhaustive and describes the product feature and marketing aspects of commodities rather than the more detailed technical aspects of their design and user effects. Some of the above characteristics can be identified as far back as the 'boom box', the Sony Walkman cassette player, portable earphones, gaming devices, portable electronic typewriters, laptop computers, and more lately, mobile phones, Personal Digital Assistants (PDAs), mini-laptops, the ubiquitous Apple iPod and now the iPhone and iPad. In-home entertainment devices are increasingly designed as body-engaging or body-extending, including surround sound, large-screen televisions, high definition image display, and multi-sensory game controllers, such as the Nintendo Wii. The overall trend is that technology engages young people in more ways, at more times and in more places: their participation is multi-sensory, multi-tasked and multi-dimensional.

The above aspects of personal embodiment include individuality, portability, sensory micro-control, sensory feedback, and technology as fashion. Indeed, these trends are undisputed by producers, marketers and media commentators. What then do these developments in technology contribute to the experience of its use? I suggest that the following experiential aspects of technology use are relevant to our discussion of both adolescent spirituality and sexuality.

Sensuality

Through both control and feedback mechanisms, technology is able to more precisely both 'read' from and 'write' to a greater range of human bodily movements and expressions (micro-sensory), more body parts with multi-sensory synchronicity, and with an exaggerated sense of reality (hyper-sensory). While over-stimulation may seem to be the resulting risk, such as with hyper-real computer games, more refined moderation of the senses is equally possible, inducing tranquility and relaxation.[42]

Intimacy

Greater sensory stimuli provide an avenue for a heightened sense of psychological intimacy—the feeling of being physically and emotionally closer to another. Such intimacy might encompass the adrenalin-sweat of a close battle in a computer game, the romantic nearness of a heart-felt music performer, or the empathic presence of an interstate chat friend. Such experiences blur distinctions between 'real' and 'virtual' in both the practices and memories of technology users, moreover they indicate emotively varied intimacies with a range of subjects. For young people, both SMS texting and online chatting enable intimate conversation due to their privacy and easy access.

Spontaneity

The miniaturisisation, increased manipulation and portability of particular technologies provide greater accessibility in terms of place, time and control. Users are able to interact physically with an increased range of devices not only more frequently, but are also able to more easily access 'on demand' the particular service or source that they seek. The result is more frequent, more impulsive, and for some, more compulsive use, as is the case with young people and mobile phones. Such capacity has behavioural effects with both social and commercial implications.

Necessity

The habitual nature of humans opens up these technological pandoras, for good or ill, from 'can' to 'will' to 'must'. Affordability with availability leads to indispensability, both in the entertainment and employment arenas. The increasing integration of ICT with entertainment content such as movies, games and website experiences is a direct attempt by global ICT corporations to make technology an integrative aspect of both leisure and

---

42. See for example, iPhone applications such as Brian Eno's *Bloom*; Grace Cathedral's online labyrinth at http://www.gracecathedral.org/labyrinth/interactions/labyrinth.shtml; and Wild Divine at http://www.wilddivine.com.

learning, particularly for children and young people. Technology may be seen as a modern panacea, yet its very ubiquity suggests a very broad and diverse multiplicity of needs and fulfillments; the design challenge for the ICT industry. Similarly, the reasons for technology use are never static for individuals or groups. Evolution is almost inevitably innate to the technological revolution.

Transcendence

Technology can extend human perception, intuition, connectivity and control beyond its immediate, imagined and sensory limits. Currently, touch-screen and motion-sensitive technologies, such as in the Nintendo Wii and the Apple iPhone and iPod Touch, clearly exhibit appeal to young people. These devices and others allow for extended, heightened or novel experiences that deepen a sense of connection to real or imagined worlds, heighten sensory experiences, and extend the capacity to control real-world events. Our tools are always, by definition, self-transcending.

Each of the above characteristics of technology invites bodily engagement, including physical, cognitive and affective interactivity. As technology requires patterned use, these characteristics inform embodied habits, repetitive practices through which young people engage in meaning-making. According to Anthony Giddens, the construction of the self is a reflexive task for people in post-traditional society.[43] The plurality of cultural structures and forms not only allows for personal choice but requires more than this; an interactive engagement in constructing meaningful and satisfying ways of life. In supporting Giddens' view, I suggest that reification, the task of assigning artefacts symbolic meaning, is an essential aspect of the use of ICT, through which the *aesthetisation* of everyday life is undertaken.[44]

Rather than seeing young people as passive, even brainwashed, consumers of electronic culture, we may instead see them as consciously assigning significance to technological practices, constantly revising their media use and its meaning, and creatively producing novel applications and interpretations. However, the active role of young people in techno-

---

43. Anthony Giddens, Modernity and Self-Identity: Self and Society in the Late Modern Age (Cambridge: Polity, 1991).
44. The term 'aestheticisation' in this context is used by Mike Featherstone, *Consumer Culture and Postmodernism* (London: Sage, 2007).

logical meaning-making often causes increased rather than reduced anxiety among parents, teachers and church leaders. To use Giddens' terms, the ontological security of teenagers within technoculture challenges the existential anxiety of their elders.

The embodiment of technology, with its sensual, sexual and spiritual dimensions, also constitutes a challenge to social norms regarding privacy, individuality, and authenticity. Having identified the 'body' as a problem in societal views of adolescence, and indicated that ICT is inextricably connected with the bodies of its users, I further suggest that media technologies are seen, both by society and by the church, as a particular danger in terms of sexuality and well-being, and therefore, a threat to spiritual development.

6. The risk of technology

In Australia and overseas, technologism has subsumed eroticism as the perceived evil threatening young people. The risks associated with young people's use of technology often encompass public concerns about adolescent sexual expression and safety. Within adults' general unease about teenage obsessions with technology is a more specific disquiet regarding their access to sexually explicit material, unwelcome advances by strangers and either naïve or perverse self-disclosure. Rather than replacing sex as the young person's temptation of choice, the electronic realm in fact encompasses and expands the perceived risks.

In popular discourses concerning ICT, these intimate and uncontrollable aspects of media technologies constitute dual dangers to young people. The mass media frequently associate the Internet with personal risks to teenagers.[45] Several studies indicate that exposure to inappropriate material such as pornography and violence is common.[46] Parents, schools

---

45. AAP, 'Internet sex groomer gets 15 months jail', http://news.theage.com.au/breaking-news-national/internet-sex-groomer-gets-15-months-jail-20091216-kw4m.html. Accessed 18 December, 2009.
46. Michelle Fleming *et al*, 'Safety in Cyberspace: Adolescents' Safety and Exposure Online', *Youth & Society*, Volume 38 Number 2 (2006): 135–154; Kimberley Mitchell *et al*, 'The Exposure of Youth to Unwanted Sexual Material on the Internet', *Youth & Society*, Volume 34 Number 3 (2003): 330–358.

and governments are in constant debate about regulating technology to restrict young people's access to websites and chat rooms.[47]

Whereas a teenager's bedroom was once a place of seclusion from the world, with broadband access it becomes an exclusive haven for unrestricted private exploration. In my teaching sessions with adults, often parents and grandparents, this concern is voiced frequently. From their perspective, technology, while desirable, seems an inevitable yet unwelcome intrusion into the personal life of a child, largely outside parental control. It is not difficult to see how adults may see media technologies as seductive and imposing, while simultaneously valuing ICT's educational benefits.

Engagement with media technology, particularly the Internet, may be seen as metaphorically sexual through its combination of sexual content, sensual interfaces, secret late night chats, interactive responses and 'private' locations. Types of 'sexual protection' are even available in the form of electronic filters, albeit with limited effectiveness![48] This is not to say that the technology is inevitably or essentially sexualised. Rather, the design trends of intimacy and universal access, combined with open entry to a world of content, are seen to allow the exploitation of young people at a time in their development when they are particularly open to sexual exploration. The Internet represents an invasive threat to a child's naïveté. As was the case in the 1950s and 1960s, sexual expression exists as a very public issue of privacy. The difference here is that sexual material is mediated and moves outside constraints of time or space.

While the sexual content of communication technologies may be acknowledged, any overlap with teenage spirituality may be less evident. However a substantial amount of research acknowledges the presence of spiritual themes within the mass media and its technologies.[49] We can see ample evidence of spiritual content in the mass media, from TV shows such as *Medium*, *Ghost Whisperer* and *Charmed* to movies such as the *Harry Potter* series and Studio Ghibli films, for example, *Spirited Away*. These two movies, along with others such as *The Golden Compass* and

---

47. Australian Communication and Media Authority (ACMA), *Click and Connect: Young Australians' Use of Online Social Media* (Melbourne: ACMA, 2009).
48. Fleming *et al*, 'Safety in Cyberspace: Adolescents' Safety and Exposure Online', *op cit*.
49. For example, Lynn Schofield Clark, *From Angels to Aliens: Teenagers, the Media and the Supernatural* (New York: Oxford University Press, 2003).

Avatar, exemplify the current trend in youth and children's films of associating the natural world with 'supernatural' powers.[50] *Avatar* combines an interspecies love story with a narrative about the protective and healing power of a 'Gaia' world, a sentient alien planet, essentially a life-force that is able to transcend even the barriers that separate people from different worlds. Entertainment media regularly present narratives with spiritual or supernatural dimensions to children and young people; indeed such media are most likely the primary means by which young people encounter mediated spirituality. Children grow up immersed in media that present them with imaginative worlds transcending everyday reality and offering supernatural narratives of hope, victory and friendship.

Studies of science fiction and fantasy/horror films indicate a strong connection between sexuality, the supernatural and the alien or outsider.[51] Sex and sexuality have long been explicit themes in science fiction films, from *Metropolis* to *Barbarella* to *Alien*. The romance in *Avatar* continues a trend in teenage film and television reaching back to *Star Trek* and beyond, of loving the alien. The *Buffy* series and now *Twilight* continue this theme in relation to the underworld of vampires. If both romance and spirituality are frequent themes in teenage entertainment, two questions arise; to what extent do young people associate spirituality and romance with the habits of use of electronic media (as distinct from their content), and to what extent to adults, who are less native to the electronic world, harbour different or opposing views?

In *Haunted Media*, Jeffrey Sconce suggests that adult fear of technology may be grounded in the evolution of new media throughout the last century,.[52] His broad study chronicles early views of electricity and the telegraph as containing spiritual presence, a rising interest in extraterrestrial communication that accompanied the spread of the radio, and the later discourse concerning television as a doorway to unreal worlds. Remember that this is the century in which the notion of 'outer space' entered our homes through the mass media. Sconce identifies an ongoing

---

50. Sarah Pike, 'Why Prince Charles Instead of "Princess Mononoke?" The Absence of Children and Popular Culture in The Encyclopedia of Religion and Nature', *Journal of the American Academy of Religion*, Volume 77 (2009): 66–72.
51. Gerard Loughlin, Alien Sex: The Body And Desire In Cinema And Theology (Oxford: Blackwell, 2004).
52. Jeffrey Sconce, *Haunted Media* (Durham: Duke University Press, 2000).

association between electronic media and the spiritual or paranormal in the US. The author notes the parallels between popular views of emerging technologies and their actual content, from Orson Welles' radio play *The War of the Worlds* to televised twilight zones.

Sconce gives evidence of public opinion that electronic technologies are alien devices opening gateways to oblivion. In his view, notions of electricity, radio waves and television transmissions as flowing or liquid are in accord with seeing human consciousness as a stream. Hence the media unlock a floodgate of information and experience in which we might dissolve. The metaphor of technology as a seeping menace is clear. Sconce's study provides a helpful historical discursor to contemporary concerns regarding the invasion of the internet into the household. Today's fifty year olds remember the introduction of television and computers, their parents grew up with the wireless and telephone. Given the pace of technological development in recent decades, the vast majority of adults have vivid memories of how new ICTs have altered home life. Whether or not adults today see technology as sinister, there is little doubt that they are aware of its power to reshape relationships and lifestyles. An implication of Sconce's study is that adults may be more likely than young people to see communication technologies as spiritually menacing rather than life-giving.

7. The promise of technology

Richard Stivers sees in the current milieu a tendency to treat technology as magic, something not fully understood by the masses but nevertheless trusted and relied upon for its services. Magic provides control of the natural world.[53] Technology as magic is imbued with symbolic power to solve all of our problems, becoming a focus for our irrational hopes and fears. Historically, magic becomes separated from religion, being more practical, individual and quasi-scientific in its application, such as expressed in the 'new age' movement. According to Stivers, while religion seems to theorise about nature, technology manipulates it. Religion becomes either a mystical escape from the problems of nature or a social projection onto a deity. Meanwhile technology takes the form of expertly-designed

---

53. Richard Stivers, *Technology as Magic* (New York: Continuum, 2001).

practices forming ritualised behaviours that shape our interactions with the natural world. Such views of technology require magical sustaining mythologies.

Stivers seeks to stand outside the fishbowl of technology in which young people are immersed. Based on Bill Gates' mythology that sees the PC and Internet with unbridled optimism, teenagers may see technology as benevolent, or more likely, as the equivalent of the car; something that is 'just there'.[54] In this regard, young people do not 'use' technology; it is an increasingly invisible aspect of their communication habits. Imagine asking most teenagers, "Do you use a mobile phone?"

For both Stivers and Sconce, the promise of technology is not wholly utopian; its invasiveness in many areas of our lives evokes hidden anxieties at the heart of human existence itself. An implication of both authors' work is that the use of technology requires acts of faith; not only the hope that our tools will do what we ask of them, but that we will not also be consumed in the process. It would be too big a leap to say that such faith is inherently spiritual. Yet, to the extent that such tools embody our hopes and fears, our technology habits may indeed foster the kinds of magical dependence that Stivers suggests.

This is worthwhile territory for further investigation. Beyond utilitarian questions regarding daily usage, to what extent does trust in technology to provide transcendent experiences engender a disposition toward 'mediated' spirituality?

7. Conclusion

Public concerns regarding teenagers and their sexual development have been subsumed and even magnified by media discourses concerning technology. Social institutions, including churches, have viewed technology as a threat to young people at the same time that they have embraced its promise for progress. These mixed messages conveyed to young people regarding technology are a continuation of cultural narratives concerning the perils of teenage sexual expression. Furthermore, the personal and social aspects of communication technologies provide for regular, intimate connectedness in ways that can relieve loneliness, invite self-disclosure,

---

54. Bill Gates, *The Road Ahead* (London: Viking, 1995).

and build trust, and may thus enable the deep knowing that human beings crave. To see the desire for intimacy and connectedness as a strong spiritual yearning, related to self-knowledge and self-transcendence, is to acknowledge ICT as a potentially significant vehicle for mediated spirituality for young people.

If we see young people's spiritual lives through the lens of bodily experience, then both immediate and mediated stimulation, including intimacy and adventure, may be more significant than researchers have recognised. Future studies will need to find data collection methods that invite young people to speak more honestly about the kinds of experiences that are intimate, risky, liminal, and transformational. Moreover, recent studies of spirituality identify the importance of relationships for young people and to some extent recognise the significance of electronic media. However, these investigations fall short of examining the ways in which the social uses of communication technologies may be spiritually significant for young people. Given teenagers' lack of a cohesive language for spiritual experience, further work is needed to explore the transcendent aspirations of their ICT usage.

If young people seek and find spiritual experiences through mediated self-transcendence, then it is critical that churches and their youth ministries investigate whether this requires a shift from the view that authenticity in relationships is limited to physical presence or real-time communication.

List of Contributors

Adam Cooper is Senior Lecturer in Patristics at the John Paul II Institute for Marriage and Family, Melbourne. He holds a PhD from Durham University (UK) and an STL from the Lateran University (Rome). He has published numerous articles and books in theology, including *Life in the Flesh* (OUP, 2008) and *The Body in Saint Maximus the Confessor* (OUP, 2005). He is currently completing a monograph on deification in modern Catholic theology.

Joanna Cruickshank is Lecturer in History at Deakin University, Victoria. She has published on eighteenth-century English evangelicalism and nineteenth-century Australian Aboriginal missions. Her current project is a co-authored book (with Professor Pat Grimshaw) on women and missions in nineteenth-century Australia.

Stephen Garner is Lecturer in Theology in the School of Theology, University of Auckland, New Zealand and holds an MSc in computer science and a PhD in theology. He currently teaches and researches in the areas of theological ethics, public and contextual theology, science, technology and religion, theology and popular culture, and spirituality. He is also a member of the New Zealand Interchurch Bioethics Council representing the Presbyterian Church of Aotearoa New Zealand.

Nicola Hoggard-Creegan is Senior Lecturer in Theology at Laidlaw College, Auckland, New Zealand and Dean of the Laidlaw-Carey Graduate School. She studied mathematics at Victoria University in Wellington, biology in Australia, and theology at Gordon Conwell and Drew University, New Jersey (PhD). She is interested in feminist theology, the science/theology interface, evolutionary theory and ecotheology. She has recently written a book, *Animal Suffering and the problem of Evil*, which she hopes will be published next year.

Craig Mitchell is Director of Christian Education and Discipleship at Uniting College for Leadership & Theology, Adelaide, South Australia, and on the faculty of the Department of Theology for Flinders University. His teaching and research is in the areas of youth ministry, Christian education and discipleship, spirituality, media and communication.

Lightning Source UK Ltd.
Milton Keynes UK
UKHW050928010421
381326UK00012B/235